WAR ON U.S.

HOW POLICIES AND PEOPLE ARE DESTROYING AMERICA

Visit www.booksurge.com to order additional copies.

WAR ON U.S.

HOW POLICIES AND PEOPLE ARE DESTROYING AMERICA

BY JOHN CHERRY

CONTENTS

INTRODUCTION

I T HAS BEEN ten years since I started this book. I never envisioned myself as a writer, and certainly the English teachers throughout my academic career would feel the same way. The impetus to write this book began initially out of frustration. Stuck behind another slow driver in the left lane of a four lane highway, I would find myself calling friends to alert them of the numerous hazards and frustrations of being on the road. These expressions began to expand to other subjects as my interest in local, national and world problems became more focused. Much has happened in the last decade. We were attacked by Al-Qaeda, lost another Beatle, spent too much on government and ridded the world of a murderous dictator and his two crazy sons. The Yankees won three World Series (it's time for some more), Carolina won a men's basketball championship and Tiger

Woods dominated the golf world. "W" won two elections over two irritating stiffs, and led us into victory on the battlefield.(I bet Nancy and Harry like that line!) As another election approaches, let's hope we elect a strong leader as we continue to face the war on terror.

To write a book like this is a mammoth undertaking, especially on your own.

The research is ongoing and the typing is slow (28 WPM). I worked a full-time job until July of 2005, then have spent two years in southwest Florida, enjoying the warm weather and the golf courses. The book was "finished"a few times, but I was unable or unwilling to pursue publication. Then, with the decks cleared, I began anew to rewrite the entire book. Adding and deleting a lot, I brought my work up to date, all the while continuing to gather research to stay current.

Based on what I have read, Glenn Beck has recently published a book that addresses a number of subjects found in my book. As I write this foreword, Beck's "An Inconvenient Book" is number one on the N.Y. Times bestsellers list. Being a competitive sort, I'd also like to be number one. Unless you are at a bookstore reading this page, I'm thinking you are helping me to get to the top. If so, I hope to see you at a book signing or other related event.

As you will note in the chapter titles, many sensitive subjects are addressed. I hope you will turn the pages with an open mind and will derive some benefit from your purchase. To those of you who do not learn anything: **YOU NEED HELP!**

"He who best understands the world, least likes it."

— Ben Franklin

CHAPTER ONE

THE TRUE REASONS FOR "ROAD RAGE"

YOU MIGHT QUESTION why I would start this book with a chapter about road rage, but I think you will understand after you read how many of the serious problems of the world are related to problems on the road.

Ten years ago, I was sitting at a stoplight on an October morning, waiting to cross one of the busiest intersections in Chapel Hill. To my left, I see heavy traffic coming toward me. A Ford Escort suddenly cuts in front of a semi-truck in the right lane. To avoid hitting the Escort, which comes to a quick stop for the light, the truck driver veers off the shoulder and is now heading to hit me broadside. I do not have time to react, and the astute truck driver deftly cuts the semi around the Escort. For a brief moment, I feel safe, but the truck is carrying a large bulldozer, secured in two places by a large chain. That security is breached in one spot when the truck veers from right to left through the intersection. The bulldozer dangles off the side of the truck enough to rip the hood and front bumper off my vehicle, flipping the hood around to the back door of the passenger side.

Since I did not see the bulldozer until after impact, I was not immediately shaken by the accident. Until I see the hood missing, I am not aware that I have narrowly escaped a potential serious injury, or even death. The truck driver was able to stop several hundred feet down the road. He gets out of his vehicle and races back to my car to check on my condition. "Are you okay, are you okay?" the driver yells to me as I slowly get out of the car. "Yes, I am okay" I reply, as I walk toward the front of the car. It comes to my realization that his alert maneuvering has saved me from a potentially serious injury. I turn to him and say "thank you for what you did." He seems puzzled, but my sentiment seems to sink in as he has a little more time to survey the scene and consider he may have avoided a disaster. By this time, the Ford Escort is on his merry way.

This is my second brush with death in a near fatal car accident, the first occurring 28 years ago, just outside Norman, Oklahoma. Just as in October, 1997, quick action by a driver likely saves my life.

For eight years, everyday on the way to work, I had a reminder about the accident. There was a lengthy groove in the payment where the blade of the hanging bulldozer carved an inch deep chunk in the asphalt. As I waited for the light to change in the morning, there was a vivid reminder of my close call with disaster.

U.S. roads are more dangerous every day, due to a variety of reasons. It is my mission to show you the causes of the danger and ideas for some solutions. First, it is the lack of experience and intelligence on the road. Age, distractions, and corruption in the licensing process are also factors.

While I would have screamed in protest if I could not get my driver's license at sixteen, I did have two accidents during my first year of driving. The licensing process for first-time drivers is slowly being revamped in the U.S., but the changes are not coming fast enough to significantly reduce the highway deaths of teenage drivers. While the graduated license (GDL) option is a promising avenue in most states, seven states and the District of Columbia continue to offer unrestricted licenses for sixteen year olds. The graduated option parcels out the responsibility to the new drivers, usually up to age eighteen, by requiring adults in the car, limiting the hours for driving, and reducing the number of occupants. The Transportation Research Board reports that the death rate for 16 year old drivers increased 51% from 1975-1996, while the rate for 17-19 year olds was down 27%. This makes a strong case for the GDL. States with well-designed GDL's saw a 20% decrease in accidents involving 16 year olds in 2006.

According to a study done jointly by the Children's Hospital of Philadelphia and State Farm Insurance, vehicle crashes are the leading cause of death for 15-20 year olds. This age group represents 6.3% of the licensed drivers on the road, but are involved in 12.6% of the fatal crashes. The young drivers are also five times as likely to be in a fatal crash when the car has two or more occupants. On an average U.S. day, **ten** of the 15-20 year olds are killed on the road, but it can be worse. On November 1, 2003, **26** from that age group were killed in 24 crashes on U.S. highways. From 1993-1997, teen drivers killed occupants of other vehicles at a rate of nearly five times as elderly drivers and three times as high as 45-49 aged drivers, according to an analysis by the Insurance Institute for Highway Safety. From 1995-2004, crashes involving drivers 15-17 years old killed nearly 31,000 people.

According to a report published in March of 2005, 77% of 16 year old fatal crashes were attributable to driver error. The state of New Jersey has long barred 16 year old drivers and has had one of the lowest teen fatality rates in the U.S. As the number of 16 year olds allowed to drive is dropping due to the increased implementation of the graduated license, the number of accidents involving those drivers has decreased proportionately.

Other countries are much more stringent about the process to obtain a drivers license. In Germany, at 18 years old, you can be taught to drive at fairly rigorous and expensive driving schools. In France, you cannot get a license until you are 18, as driver training runs from 16-18 years of age.

I especially like the British laws, where you can get a provisional license at 17, but you must drive with someone 21 years or older. Also, best of all, the young driver must display red "L" plates on the car they are driving. I would think that these red plates might be effectively used to designate other "high-risk" drivers as well. If I had my way with this idea, they might run out of red plates, due to slow, inattentive and just bad drivers.

The age factors also show up in the fact that the part of the brain that weighs risks and controls isn't fully developed until age 25. Attitudes and emotions are the biggest factors.

The American public favors the restricted licensing, evidenced by the fact that a CNN/USA Today/Gallup Poll indicated that 61% of those polled believed 16 is too young for a license, and 53% think 18 should be the magic age.

Although I might be banned from Florida for this part of the book, it is also necessary to examine the other end of the age spectrum on the driving issue. In October of 2005, about an hour from my residence, a 93 year old hit a man, but did nothing, driving for miles with part of the body hanging out of the windshield. A stop at a toll booth brought the tragedy to an end. Elderly drivers (75+ years) are more likely to be involved in fatal crashes at traffic intersections than are younger (16-24 years) drivers, according to the Insurance Institute for Highway Safety. By 2030, the number of licensed drivers aged 65 and older will nearly double to 57 million-nearly one in five drivers. Those same drivers are expected to account for 16% of all crashes and 25% of fatal crashes by that time.

The General Accounting Office (GAO) reports that only 16 states demand that seniors undergo more frequent license renewals than non-seniors. Only five states require older drivers to renew their license in person, and only New Hampshire and Illinois require road tests for those 75 years and older. Threatening to remove or restrict driving privileges is very stressful to the elderly. Perhaps requiring an AARP type of driving refresher course would be a better way to go" said Charles "Doc" Anderson, Republican congressman from Waco, TX. I, and many of you, know what "Doc" is saying. My father, despite being in the early to middle stages of Alzheimers, did not want to give up driving. Even though he only took trips to a few local locations, he did get lost one day and was rescued by a Durham, NC realtor that looked at his license after he pulled off the road, and then drove him home. After that incident, he never seemed interested in driving again. Our family was lucky, and I am sure many of you have heart breaking stories of how your parents were taken off the road.

The issue of older drivers should be handled in a delicate manner. Our senior drivers deserve to be treated with compassion, so the choice of solutions should strike a balance between safety and maintaining their lifestyle. The AAA Foundation for Traffic Safety suggests that drivers 55 years and older with poor driving records should be required to take driver education courses designed for them. The courses should be readily available for the seniors. Additionally, road tests should be required for drivers over 70 years old. Seniors should be required to take periodic vision exams for acuity, depth perception and peripheral vision. At present, Virginia does not require these tests until the age of 80.

For those unable or unwilling to drive, there is a need for assistance. In Portland, Maine, ITN America has drivers available 24 hours a day. The average fee is $8 per trip. Cars can be traded in for trip credit. This idea has been bolstered by the "Older Americans Sustainable Mobility Act," sponsored by Susan Collins, R-Maine, in February 2006. Some states and communities are not waiting for the federal support. Connecticut is following Maine's plan and Rhode Island is considering one. Paid and volunteer drivers provide the transportation, and Portland's plan provided over 15,000 trips in 2005. Instead of swallowing their pride and asking the same friends and family for rides, this type of option can provide the seniors both dignity and adequate transportation. The idea for ITN came from a mother whose daughter nearly lost her life in an accident involving an 84 year old driver.

While the oldest and youngest drivers are a significant factor in the overall problem on the roads, there are other factors to consider as well. First, there is the immigration issue. Due to the influx from our southern borders, there has been too much catering to the illegals from Mexico and other southern countries. Eight states, including North Carolina, allow undocumented immigrants to obtain driver licenses. Congress has legislated a

May, 2008 deadline on the licensing, but some states are still resisting. Driver's license exams should be taken in English only, otherwise the road signs may not be read correctly. Only six states are limiting their license tests to English only.

Corrupt Department of Motor Vehicles' (DMV) offices in a number of states are putting additional "at risk" drivers on the road. In Florida, DMV officials sold drivers licenses for $100-$200 to more than two thousand people, some of whom used their illegal license to drive 18 wheelers without truck training and haul hazardous materials. The licenses allowed several illegal immigrants to claim US citizenship, and eleven of those were involved in car crashes, one with a fatality. Twenty-nine faced immigration charges, including a number from Middle East countries.

Lest we forget, nine of the nineteen 9-11 hijackers had driver's licenses from Florida. DMV offices in Durham, NC have seen several cases of licenses being sold for cash or drugs. The same problem has surfaced in California, New York, and Illinois. The accusations of payoffs reached all the way to the governor's office in Illinois. Federal prosecutors secured 43 convictions or guilty pleas in the "Operation Safe Road" investigation. The inspector general was charged with blocking investigations into the scheme, concealing evidence and lying to the FBI. The Secretary of State, Richard Juliano (note the last name ending with a vowel) was convicted. Investigators say the licenses-for-sale scheme funneled at least $170,000 into Governor Ryan's 1998 campaign fund. Mercifully, Ryan did not run for re-election. In California, with the large Hispanic influx, 80% of recent license-fraud cases have involved illegal immigrants. California does require, unlike most other states, that an applicant prove legal residence of the U.S. before a license can be acquired. Former California governor Grey Davis, a disaster in office before being recalled, and the heavily Democrat Legislature tried to change this requirement. Eighty motor vehicle clerks were fired in California for taking bribes over an 18-month period from January 1996. Authorities believe thousands of fraudulent licenses were issued. In New York, at least 134 workers in the New York DMV were arrested over an eight year period; one office in New York City had to close for a day when 35 employees were busted. Of course, the most serious payoffs involved possible suspects in the terrorist's attacks. In Tennessee, an examiner caught selling licenses to some "towel heads" was blown up in her car just before her scheduled testimony.

With the large percentage of Hispanics and Asians in California, you have two populations with differing driving difficulties. The Hispanics, usually driving in clusters, are used to bumper car mentality from driving in Mexico. While working on this book, there were three massive traffic accidents in the Research Triangle Park, NC area, all involving a group of Hispanics in old vans. The Asians, with the apparent peripheral vision problems according to legal sources in California, are often involved in accidents as a result of these problems. I personally find that most of them drive too slow and have tunnel vision.

Cell phones have become another negative road factor. On May 13, 2005 USA Today ran an editorial titled "Yes, a cell phone can make you a menace on the road." "Hang up and drive, you #**!" is a sentiment many drivers have expressed while trying to avoid motorists oblivious to anything but their imperative cell phone connection. The editorial also noted using the cell phone made the driver four times as likely to get into crashes with serious injuries, according to the Insurance Institute for Highway Safety. Based on accident data, the study also noted that hands-free use of phones was only slightly safer. A Harvard study links cell phones to about 6% of annual highway deaths and 12% of the injuries. AAA Go Magazine released a survey that stated "Concerning the use of hand-held cell phones while driving, 81% in South Carolina and 79% in North Carolina said it should be against the law- a position endorsed by AAA Carolinas." Surprisingly, 54% in South Carolina and 50% in North Carolina even favored a ban on hands-free cell phone use in the car. I guess many other people are also seeing that bad drivers plus increased distraction only increases the danger on the road. The results were from an annual survey of AAA Carolinas members. A recent poll by AAA Auto Club South showed that more than 83% favored no electronic communication while driving, while 70% favored prohibiting the use of cell phones while driving.

It would seem that more comprehensive driving tests are needed, obvious stricter control of the license procurement process and a crackdown on simply poor driving. In a letter to "USA Today," a source of much of the previous information on the license selling and traffic safety, Gary Martin of Gahanna, Ohio wrote that a previous article on "road rage" had failed to note the two "major" causes 1.) Slow drivers who won't yield to faster traffic in passing lanes. 2.) Unreasonably low speed limits. Martin notes that there have been several incidents of people arrested for "road rage" and in almost every case the incidents never would have happened if selfish, stubborn drivers hogging the passing lane allowed faster traffic to pass. Going further, Martin believes there are too many people on the road who think it's OK to drive five to ten miles below the speed limit in the passing lanes, while 15 others playing traffic cop attempt to keep traffic from going faster than the speed limit, by intentionally blocking the flow of traffic exceeding the limit. If we are honest, we'd conclude these wannabe cops and oblivious drivers are creating much more of a traffic hazard than those traveling a few miles above the speed limit. The next time it happens to you, look at the long lines of densely packed traffic behind you for confirmation. While mentioning that unreasonably low speed limits choke off the flow of traffic, Martin makes the terrific suggestion of making the blocking of the passing lane a ticketed offense in every state and aggressively enforcing it.

Along with alcohol, ignorance and speed, the license renewal process must be overhauled. Writing for the "Waco Tribune-Herald," Senior Editor Rowland Nethaway succinctly stated, "The best way to make the U.S. streets and highways safer is to have better drivers." Nethaway had taken a European-style driver's test from a Bermudian officer. Passing Rowland with a stern lecture, the officer talked about the need to accurately judge speed, keep up with the flow of traffic, and execute evasive maneuvers and other skills never tested in the U.S. In addition to the lecture, the officer gave Nethaway his opinion of U.S. drivers. "Americans are the worst drivers in the world. They depend on their politicians to keep them safe rather than their driving skills. Europeans emphasize driving skills first and government regulations last." Following his difficult test, Rowland had the following opinion: "Our country hands out driver licenses as though driving is a right rather than a privilege. The licensing process is an unfunny joke. Poke around a few blocks, parallel-park and pass a dumbed-down multiple-choice quiz. You are licensed to kill. Does that make any sense?" Rowland's conclusion- "American motorists should be required to pass driving tests similar to those administered to pilots and motorists in many European nations. Physical exams should also be required."

The significant growth in congestion on our highways in many areas, including locally, is also a major factor in both "road rage" and traffic accidents. I am amazed at the length of time necessary to complete new roads. My gut feeling is that the road-building business is a "rigged game" with only so many players, an overweight bureaucracy is often involved and the environmental extremists have created additional red tape. I do find it interesting that South Carolina was able to compress 27 years of road building into seven years, mixing state, federal and hospitality funds to accelerate completion. Is there any reason why this cannot be done everywhere? Congestion is also a result of growth and urban sprawl, a subject for another chapter that hits right at home. Pick up your daily newspaper and the police blotter will often include a drunk driver without any license or a revoked license, either in a wreck or just caught DWI. Our Spanish-speaking friends are often the culprit and I suspect this is true throughout much of the U.S., where immigration is overwhelming us. Also, as usual, you will see others arrested who are "victims" of one overstated excuse or another.

Whereas immigration must be controlled more efficiently, we must also make a concerted effort to drive corruption out of the driver license procurement process. The tests should be thorough on a written and road test basis. After age 60, the driving test should be required every four years. Discrimination? No, it is safety. The number of lives lost on the highway can be reduced significantly with these changes in the present system. Other ideas should also be pursued, perhaps to include stricter penalties for violators on the road without a proper license.

According to an AAA Foundation study, unlicensed drivers were involved in 20% of the U.S. fatal crashes from 1993-1997. In North Carolina, 40% of those in fatal crashes had had their license suspended or revoked three or more times in the three previous years. There are many warning signs to look for on the road. I start with the make of the vehicle. The worst cars on the road to be behind (particularly in the left lane of an interstate or four-lane highway) are Ford Escort, Dodge Neon, Lincoln Continental, Mercury Marquis and the "Nemesis". Be careful around any vehicle with dark or tinted glass, ugly colors of puke green, bright red or lavender, or an old Buick with more than four passengers. Actually, in Florida, it is just about any Buick-moving too damn slow!!

"Nemesis" vehicles are mini-vans, or often just vehicles of the same size. The mini-van has replaced the station wagon as the most likely vehicle to be driving slowly where the driver is distracted, unable to pay attention, or generally just a bad driver. On two-lane roads, it is very difficult to see around "Nemesis" vehicles, making it difficult to pass, which is usually necessary. Based on my observations, there are many "soccer moms" in these vehicles, making bad decisions on the road and uninformed decisions at the ballot box.

There are other warning signs on the road. If you see a car with a cracked windshield, beware of a bad driver. Why? I'd guess the car was in an accident and the people are afraid of using their insurance company. Can't afford it? There is a process available that basically "sucks" the crack out of the glass, leaving only an indistinguishable hole. The cost is only $50-$100. Also look for a "vanity" license plate, especially those with reference to the driver's name. The "my son or daughter is an honor student at some school" sticker, particularly from the Kiwanis club, seems to be a near lock for potential trouble; I guess the parents are so shocked that their child has done well that they have to publicize it. I would say that with today's schools, it is likely that the kid isn't that intelligent and neither are the parents, which translates to poor judgment on the road.

Multiple stickers also pinpoint a poor driver; perhaps they are more interested in making a statement or making themselves feel better. Just like the numerous bumper stickers, the Fish emblem usually guarantees a poor driver. The "Religion and Tradition" chapter will further explain the reliance on religion, but the "crutch" factor normally means these people have difficulty making decisions and living their "own" life. On the road, this translates into slow decision making and driving. Other warnings are dice hanging from the rearview mirror, Christmas tree and crown air fresheners, drivers who slump to the middle of the front seat, and cars with illuminated license plates and those with a chain around the rim of the plate.

The worst drivers on the road are old black women, followed by middle-aged black women, old white women, and coming up fast are the Asians and the Hispanics. This information was provided by the renowned Dr. W.W. Schlagle, Director of the Department of Transportation and Natural Resources (an ultra-secret government organization).

OK, you have finished one chapter. Are you saying, "Are you off your rocker.......John?"

Please note that the paragraph about the worst drivers was written with tongue in cheek.

CHAPTER TWO

THE INVASION OF AMERICA – PART ONE "BIN AND THE TOWEL HEADS"

September 11, 2001

I HATE ADDING THAT date to this book. Blame? I hate to point fingers, but the purpose of this book is to address the issues.

First, we let ourselves be duped by the liberal Democrats into thinking we could live by appeasement in an ever dangerous world. Many in the Clinton administration seemed content to let U.S. superiority diminish during their eight years in the White House. This was accented by the handling of the Iraqi weapons inspections, and the tepid responses to the World Trade Center bombing, embassy bombings, and the attack on the USS Cole in Yemen. However, during impeachment, Clinton did bomb a pill factory in Sudan.

Despite defending many Muslims in the Gulf War, Bosnia, and Somalia, we apparently pissed off the king of the "towel heads," Osama Bin Laden. Bolstered by their defeat of the backwards Russian army over a ten-year period, again aided by U.S. support, Bin Laden and members of the Taliban took it upon themselves to begin striking at the United States after the Gulf War. Blaming U.S. support of Israel, Bin Laden and other "cells" of terrorists declared war on the U.S. with their suicidal attacks on September 11th.

Has our response been appropriate? Until now, I say yes, with some reservations. The military campaign took less than six weeks in aiding the Northern Alliance in the takeover of most of Afghanistan. The Taliban has attempted to regroup, aided by funding from the sale of opium, but allied forces have held their ground in large part.

In Iraq, where most Republicans AND Democrats believed that Saddam Hussein had weapons of mass destruction prior to the invasion, the early military campaign was, indeed, a "mission accomplished." The aftermath faced roadblocks. One was trying to fight off the insurgents with a smaller than necessary force. John McCain spoke early of the need for more forces, but Defense

Secretary Don Rumsfeld , "Rummy," felt otherwise. He has been proven wrong by the success of the surge started in the summer of 2007. It was also not reasonable to expect the many factions inside Iraq to instantly accept a change to democracy, especially the former supporters of Saddam. Secondly, Bin Laden and Al Qaeda saw a chance, with help from Iran and Syria, to gather significant numbers of terrorists with their largely cowardly roadside and suicide bombs to disrupt the establishment of the new Iraq government. The brave and dedicated U.S. forces, along with the support of many other countries, have made tremendous progress to help the Iraqis, and a new day may be dawning for the Middle East. I think we ought to look in Syria for some WMD's shipped from Iraq, and Saddam did show all signs of supporting terrorism.

The many murders and gassing of his own people were proof that the crazed man found in a spider hole needed to be removed, and then hung. Now, what do we do to prevent future attacks? The drug money supporting the Taliban can be reduced by using the opium to make fuel. Paying the farmers for their opium crop would have the two-fold benefit of the fuel and taking the money out of the pockets of those that would support the terrorists. Just as in the corruption in Mexico, Columbia, and many other South American countries has been maintained by the influence of drug trafficking, the opium in Afghanistan has supported the evil leadership of the Taliban. The crop purchase would hit at the heart of the terror financing

As you will read in Invasion, Part Two, I have numerous recommendations to stop the influx of those who "poison" our society. Number one is to guard all of our borders. Too many people have already illegally gotten into our country. Several of the 9-11 hijackers were in the U.S. illegally and the others had used numerous aliases. Student visas were used, but there was no tracking of them, or enforcement of the visa time limit. These "holes' in our borders have to be eliminated. I mean the border with Canada, especially Mexico, and our ports. Rigid enforcement of the borders is an absolute necessity. While I abhor increased government spending, if Congress does not have the discipline to make cuts to fund these changes for security, then the additional funds should be allocated.

Our focus should be to continue smoking out the terrorists, destroying the "cells" and sending a clear message that we will maintain a strong stance against terrorism. New York City, while moving a bit slow on rebuilding the twin towers, has rebounded strongly to send the world a signal that internal security is in place.

Not surprisingly, Paul McCartney stepped up to aid the families who lost loved ones in the attacks in New York. The concert for New York City on October 20th, 2001 at Madison Square Garden consisted of the greatest lineup in musical history. Ticket sales alone accounted for nearly 15 million dollars, and a video and compact disc of the show added to the total. For your information,

Hillary nearly got booed off the stage during her introduction at the show. Smart crowd.

Many comments made by terrorists have suggested our country lacked the will to fight back, and that resolve has been tested. Certainly, the actions of towns like Berkeley, CA to condemn the U.S. military campaigns, as well as campus demonstrations (including my alma mater in Chapel Hill) give the impression that our country does not have the will to stand up to a prolonged war. Due to many factors, including some internal destruction of the U.S. intelligence community, the numerous "cells" of terrorists will take some time to destroy.

This book began by stating the reason why I felt compelled to put my ideas, opinions, and research on paper. That reason was that I felt there were too many issues that had not been dealt with in a direct manner, and these avoidances would haunt us. Our haunting soared on the morning of September 11th.

OUR WAR ON TERROR

Osama Bin Laden-"Death is better than living on this earth with the unbelievers among us."

Chief of Al Qaeda in Iraq-Abu Muzab Zarqawi- "Killing the infidels is our religion, slaughtering them is our religion, until they convert to Islam or pay us tribute."

CHAPTER TWO— PART TWO

THE INVASION OF AMERICA "HEY PEDRO, STAY ON YOUR SIDE OF THE BORDER"

WHILE "BEGINNING" THIS book, I took a Thanksgiving week vacation to the Dominican Republic. It was the opportunity to get away to a warm location as the weather began to get cold at home. Having always loved being at the beach, and having part ownership in a beach house, I thrive in the opportunity to sunbathe in late November.

Fast-talkers have always worried me, and perhaps others, why else are used-car salesman, or salespeople in general, depicted as "fast-talkers?" While acknowledging a near complete absence of the Spanish language (and most others) in my repertoire, I have a deep concern about "Spanish speakers." Besides the vocal speed, there are other reasons. Why can't the Mexican government stop its corruption and abuse of human rights? (I do have some hope for President Calderon). The greed of drug money continues to prevent the country from a change to become a major player in the world.

The United States has furnished military helicopters, modern weapons, and plenty of money to help the Mexican government attempt to fulfill it's obligations under the bogus "drug certification" policy. The corruption in the military and civilian government is so deep that the flow of drugs remains unabated. Two of Mexico's largest banks agreed in March of 2000 to forfeit over $13.5 million and pay fines of one million dollars for laundering money. The charges were based on information supplied by the U.S. drug informants posing as drug traffickers. The country has reached the point where it must decide who is running the country-drug barons or the Mexicans themselves.

The drug trafficking rings in Mexico are in the forefront of the flow of much of the cocaine, heroin, and marijuana into the United States. It is estimated by the United Nations that 90% of the cocaine sold in the U.S. comes from Mexico, and it is also the largest foreign supplier of marijuana. The trafficking has increased corruption, organized crime is involved and violent crime has spiked as a result.

Urban centers are the crime hot spots, and the economic polarization has spread the crime to the lower income earners. Minimal apprehension and conviction rates help maintain the cycle of violence and crime.

More important to the U.S., the crime problem has come across the border. Yes, I acknowledge many hard working and law abiding (except for the part about crossing the border) Mexicans come to the U.S. and are productive members of society. **BUT,** the other problems brought across the border outweigh the productive workers. Gangs, including the dreaded MS-13 group from El Salvador, are now showing up all over the United States. Towns and cities all over our country that just a few years ago thought they were gang free are now finding themselves dealing with the death, crime and drugs that are created by these groups of what I define as "domestic terrorists."

Sadly, we were warned this was coming. In the late 90's, a DEA (Drug Enforcement Administration) international operations chief warned a Senate Panel that the blood in the drug wars could spill over the border. The number of border drug-related cases more than doubled from 1995 to 1999, and continues to be a major issue for both countries.

The Mexican drug cartels also have ties to the near lawless country of Colombia. In addition to the drugs, a general sense of "lawlessness" has come across the border. Check out the local police blotters, and note the high percentage of Spanish names.

Little wonder, when down South assault and theft run rampant, and rape is rarely reported or even punished.

According to Mary Jordan of the Washington Post, the penalties for rape in some rural areas of Mexico may consist of a few hours in jail, or a minor fine.

The Center for Latin American Studies reports that high levels of corruption exist in the police, judiciary, and the government in general. Just as we have seen in Iraq, the corruption is a serious obstacle to a stable democracy. The problems are worst along the border, where some police are protecting the drug traffickers and using the law to support them.

Hope? Business leaders in Mexico City hired the security consulting company of Rudy Guiliani in 2003 to create a plan to clean up the city. In June of 2004, over 250,000 people marched through the capital and other cities to protest the failure of federal and local governments to control crime. In early 2006, in response to a rise in crime in the border region of Tijuana, Mayor Jorge Hank Rhon instituted a major technology update to the city's police force that included surveillance equipment, handheld computers, and alarm systems.

Every opinion poll over the last 20-40 years has shown that a large majority of Americans of all classes and ethnic backgrounds want less immigration. These polls have proven correct, evidenced in the grassroots reaction by the American public against the attempted immigration bills in the summer of 2007 that would, at least partially, grant amnesty to many illegal immigrants.

Why has our government let this problem grow to such enormity? Greed, power, and trying to buy votes. The cheap labor of agribusiness is a major reason. Tyson, a major contributor to another crook named Bill Clinton, was charged with conspiring to recruit and smuggle undocumented workers from Mexico to work in its processing plants. Former Tyson employee Amador Anchando-Rascon was arrested and named as the leader of a smuggling ring. He was also charged with providing ID's and social security cards. Amador had met with undercover agents and asked them to supply a plant with 2,000 illegal aliens. Besides feeding the greed of corporations, the newcomers provide a steady stream of a new underclass that keeps bureaucrats, social workers, health care specialists, bilingual educators, culture sensitivity coaches, etc. in business and power.

The past history of immigration is a story of blending into the culture of America. The visitors from south of the border appear to have different plans. In the Texas town of El Cenizo, an already divided America has developed. Spanish has been adopted as the official language and town meetings are spoken in Spanish. A resolution was adopted to state that the U.S. Border Patrol is not welcome, and any city employee caught helping the patrol could be fined. The flag of Mexico flew over city hall. Let me be blunt. It is simply un-American for an American town to declare a Mexican identity.

Several years ago, our most populated state, California, received a statement from Mario Obledo, co-founder of the Mexican American Legal Defense Fund. He told an interviewer that "one day soon his comrades will control California's political institutions, and any gringo who doesn't like it should vamoose, pronto." Now, we are going to let a Mexican tell us to leave one of our own states? Perhaps, Mario should be sent down southo.

There you have some examples of our southern friends not making the best effort to "blend" into our culture. But, there are some alarming statistics that clearly show why immigration is such an issue with the American public. In September of last year, the New Century Foundation released the following information:

50% of Hispanic households use some form of welfare, the highest of any population group.

Hispanics are 3.3 times more likely to be in prison than whites, 4.2 more times likely to be in prison for murder, and 5.8 more times more likely for felony drug charges. Young Hispanics are 19 more times more likely than whites to be in youth gangs than whites.

Hispanics drop out of high school at three times the rate of whites and twice the black rate.

The average 12th grade Hispanic reads and does math at the level of an average white 8th grader.

At 43%, the Hispanic illegitimacy rate is twice that of whites and Hispanic women have abortions at 2.7 times the white rate.

Hispanics are three more times likely than whites not to have medical insurance, and die from AIDS and tuberculosis at three times the white rate.

In California, the cost of free medical care for illegal aliens forced 60 hospitals to close from 1993 to 2003.

In Los Angeles in 2004, 95% of the 1,200-1,500 outstanding homicide warrants were issued against illegal aliens. Up to 2/3 of the 17,000 outstanding fugitive felony warrants were for illegal immigrants.

Stephen Camarota of the Center for Immigration Studies prepared research indicating that each Mexican costs the U.S. economy $55,000 over a lifetime because of lower taxes collected and more use of government as a whole. This number does not take into account the "giant sucking sound" of $20+ billion dollars that is sent, mostly wired, to Mexico from the illegals working in the U.S.

The best estimates are that Hispanics account for about 78% and Mexicans for 56% of the roughly 11 million illegal immigrants in the U.S.

Section 110 of the Illegal Immigration Reform and Immigrant Responsibility Act was to initiate an automated system to track entry and exit of all non-citizens. Implementation of the act was delayed. It is estimated that the number of illegal immigrants is at least equal to the number of legal immigrants. What a shame, but just like an area is consumed and blighted by growth, the same occurs when the population mix is not managed.

We are allowing our politicians to ignore the popular opinion. As Thomas Friedman describes it, we have become "a society where political factions become so polarized and consumed with hatred of each other that they would not let any law, any notion, constrain their behavior." While this situation seemed to start with the "New Deal" days of Franklin Roosevelt, it was a central function of the Clinton-Gore method of governing.

IT IS TIME FOR A NATIONAL ID CARD

While I reviewed the problems caused by lax and corrupt procedures at many drivers license bureaus across the country in the first chapter, the terrorist's attacks clearly pointed to the necessity of a national identification card. Eighteen of the 19 hijackers had licenses from Virginia, Florida or New Jersey, enabling the mass murderers to blend into society. The statewide driver licenses programs were not coordinated, allowing the purchases of licenses in multiple states. This is in addition to the lax systems for proof of identity. This makes it easy to get any number of different, legitimate-looking aliases in America, and makes it nearly impossible to trace those who enter the country illegally or overstay their visas. Here is some irony for you: In Mexico, all 31 states, along with the federal district of Mexico, require foreigners to present a valid visa if they want a license. Mexican officials said the rules were strictly enforced, especially in southern states that have problems with illegal immigration from Central America.

The public clearly supports some type of stricter license standards, according to a poll by the American Association of Motor Vehicle Administrators. The national survey found that 77% of Americans favor legislation to standardize state license procedures, allow cross-checking of records and boost fines for driver license fraud.

Dan Stein of the Federation for American Immigration Reform said, "If we allow someone who is here illegally and cannot prove who they are to obtain a driver's license, then we are no more secure……..than we were on September 10th."

The national ID card provides a multiple win for our country. Unauthorized drivers are reduced, illegal aliens, and the threats and problems that arrive with many of them, are reduced. This will make our country safer from terrorism, bad driving, and the increased demand on our government services. By the way, George Will had a column today (12-12-07), stating that 80% of Americans favor a national ID card. Guess who's against it?

LETTERS FROM AMERICA

"Regarding the recent story about new immigration steps and state industries' worries about labor shortages: Where were the statistics about the extreme cost of illegal immigrants as opposed to some small, in comparison, concocted benefit? What about the cost of giving illegals and their offspring "free" medical and educational benefits? Then there are the high cost of crimes such as murder, rape, theft, drug sales/smuggling, drunk driving, driving without a license and uninsured accidents often associated with illegals. People who are here illegally have no respect for our rule of law. Who would even think of giving them amnesty? In a sense, illegals have broken into our house, and we need to send them back where they came from. Who do the industry people think they are fooling? They can get all the foreign workers they want, using temporary visas. What they probably don't want is having to pay documented workers the wages they are required by law to pay. I suspect some industries live off the undocumented workers by padding their own wallets. This would be a federal crime. I suspect that some employers know full well that they are employing illegal workers, and do so while putting a tax burden on our backs. Don't fall for their worries about labor shortages."

DAVID STERLING-Venice, FL

"I welcome anyone from another country who wishes to become a good, tax paying U.S. citizen and who enters via the legal routes. But don't try to intimidate me by pulling a work stoppage or demonstration. Don't sing our national anthem in a foreign language to "strengthen your case." I find it arrogant that those who have entered our country illegally have the gall to demand that we change our laws. If you don't want to become part of our culture and language and give back to our nation, or to obey our laws, including immigration laws-then don't come in."

WILLIAM WALKER-Centerville, OH

"We are a nation of laws. I take offense at the suggestion that we must somehow extend citizenship to illegal immigrants because to do so otherwise is too hard. Illegal immigrants are a group whose presence in this country is predicated on their disdain for and violation of our laws. As a nation, we should once again choose to do what's hard, not what's easy."

MIKE DWYER-Baxley, OH

"Perhaps the dream of staying in the USA has died for many children of illegal immigrants, but the fault doesn't rest with the U.S. government. It rests with the parents who entered the USA illegally.

I don't believe we are going to deport the millions of illegal immigrants en masse, but we do have the capability to prompt an exodus through attrition. All the U.S. government has to do is enforce the laws, and illegal immigrants will return to their homelands. Attempts to control illegal immigration simply mean enforcing laws, not looking down upon all those who are less fortunate.

I'm amazed at the number of people who naively believe that we simply can ignore illegal immigration. Without controlling its borders, a nation cannot call itself sovereign."

ED CARD-Salem, SC

WHAT ABOUT U.S. SECURITY?

"It is disgraceful that the illegal immigrants fanatics-who have no regard whatsoever for our national security, the rule of law, or the welfare of 300 million Americans-want an unlimited, unregulated amount of immigrants to be allowed to enter the USA.

Illegal immigration already costs the U.S. taxpayers billions of dollars yearly-not to mention the lost wages resulting from illegal immigrants taking jobs at the lower end of the economic ladder. Illegal immigration lowers the wage scale and hurts the middle class. It is a major cause of overpopulation in our country and cannot continue without serious, detrimental and irreparable harm to life as we know it in the USA."

GREG HORAK-Aurora, CO

"Those who leave their homeland to escape abuses of human rights should instead fight for the human rights there. Their nations should begin creating programs to provide education and skills to provide for future employment, instead of creating future revolutionaries and misfits. Their government shouldn't seek a quick solution by exporting their problems across the border."

FRANK ALFONSO-Frederick, MD

"The tragedy befallen the Phillip Scott Gardner family should have never happened.

A young father of two, in the prime of his life, is dead. His wife, the young mother, is lying unconscious in critical condition in the hospital. The lives of their two young children are now dramatically altered forever.

This is the result of the (alleged) actions of an illegal immigrant. This is the result of the actions of an illegal immigrant who was (allegedly) driving while drunk.

This is the result of an illegal immigrant who has been arrested and charged twice previously with DWI!

But how is it possible that a confirmed illegal, who has habitually broken the law, remains here?

Why hadn't Ramiro Gallegos been expelled after his previous illegal actions? Ramiro Gallegos should not have been driving on

Highway 130 on July 16th (2005). Ramiro Gallegos should not have been in North Carolina on July 16th. Ramiro Gallegos should not have been in this country on July 16th."

DON GLANDER-Brunswick Beacon

"Here's why it is a problem. It's a double standard. You can't expect Americans to abide by the law while allowing illegal aliens to ignore the law. When you add up the costs for health care, schooling, free lunches, cops and courts, wouldn't it be cheaper to deport aliens, or to stop them from coming to begin with?

Some costs come in more than dollars. Scott Gardner's death on 7-16 was preventable. But it wasn't prevented."

Ramiro Gallegos criminal record:

7-15-00 Charged, later convicted in Michigan for operating vehicle while under influence of alcohol

2-02 DWI in Shallotte, NC 88 MPH in 55 MPH zone-did not appear in court. Less than a month later, North Myrtle Beach, SC police charged him with DWI after driving into lanes on US 17 and crashing into a SUV.

12-02 DWI Duplin County, NC

1-04-DWI Supply, NC

Convicted in last two cases

SMART POLITICIANS??

Rep. Walter Jones, D-N.C.-"Right now, North Carolina, the entire nation in fact, faces a tremendous economic and national security threat. A threat created by the nationwide illegal immigrant crisis." 11-05

Rep. Sue Myrick, R-N.C.-"Illegal immigrants cost our nation $15 billion last year. They account for more than 25% of America's prison population. Taxes, taxes, taxes." 11-05

DUMB POLITICIANS??

"Twice recently, outraged Americans have stopped Congress from granting amnesty to more than 12 million illegal aliens. We don't want that to happen!

But using the same lies they used back in 1986, when they stuck us with amnesty for more than a million illegal aliens, Congress is again saying, just this one time and we'll never ask again, we'll shore up the security of our borders and we'll make aliens abide by the laws of the land. This new congressional assault is hardly a surprise. American businesses want the cheap labor of aliens, legal or not, and our Congress is trying too hard to keep it for them!

Sen. Arlen Specter, ranking Republican on the Senate Judiciary Committee, is singing that old, sweet song while ramping up for the next try: "The main objective in legalizing the 12 million is to eliminate their fugitive status, allowing them to live in the United States without fear of being detected and deported."

But that is exactly what the law is supposed to do: Find all the illegal aliens and get them out of our country!

Senators Specter, John McCain, Mel Martinez, Bill Nelson, etc., must understand that supporting amnesty for an army of Mexican invaders will bring surprises at the polls next time around!"

GEORGE H.S. SHYROCK-Englewood, FL

LAWLESS COUNTRIES?

"USA Today exposed great treachery on the part of our neighbors south of the border in the article "Discount airlines fly migrants to U.S. border" (News, Oct. 12, 2007). The new discount airline in Mexico-called *Aeromigrante,* or "Migrant Air" by passengers-has been taking passengers from Central America and southern Mexico to cities along the U.S. Border, such as Tijuana and Mexicali, to assist them in their illegal entry into the USA. It is a booming one-way industry, as the article says, return flights are nearly empty. This is happening at the acquiesce of the Mexican government, a country known for its draconian immigration laws. Mexican President Felipe Calderon's puppets in Congress and the White House continue their servile obedience and work tirelessly to pass bills that smell of amnesty. The invasion continues."

PETER DILORENZO-Bonaire, GA

DOES THIS SCARE YOU?

The nation's largest intelligence training center changed security measures in May 2007 after being warned that Islamic terrorists with the aid of Mexican drug cartels were planning an attack on the facility. The alert warned that 60 Afghan and Iraqi terrorists were smuggled into the U.S. through underground tunnels with high powered weapons to attack Fort Huachuca, AZ. An FBI report claimed that "a portion of the operatives" were already in the U.S. and they had "already shaved their beards so as not to appear to be Middle Easterners."

CHAPTER THREE

"THE NEW DEAL, THE "REVERENDS" AND THE "GREAT SOCIETY"

ROM FRIENDS COAST-TO-COAST, I hear that the Mexicans are taking the jobs that the blacks, African-Americans, whatever they want to be called this year, will not do. When will certain blacks, African-Americans?, get the chip off their shoulder, as if something is now owed to them? How many races have been discriminated against in the history of our planet? There are many of them. Race relations have little chance of improving significantly as long as the chip remains, and blacks, African-Americans allow Louis Farrakan and the other "Reverends" Jesse Jackson and Al Sharpton to front themselves as voices for their race. I have spoken with two executives from companies charged with racism in the 90's who both said they were offered to have their cases disappear if substantial cash was paid to one of those "voices." Remember the Dennys and Texaco cases?

Old reliable, Professor Walter Williams, hits the bulls eye on this issue. While discussing the call of the NAACP to have more blacks in leading roles on television, Williams focuses on the actions of then President Kwesi Mfume and the "Reverend" Jackson. Early last century, Booker T. Washington warned against the agenda of "problem profiteers," proclaiming "there is a class of colored people who make a business of keeping the troubles, the wrongs and the hardships of the Negro race before the public.

Having learned that they are able to make a living out of their troubles, they have grown into the settled habit of advertising their wrongs partly because they want sympathy and partly because it pays. Some of these people do not want the Negro to lose his grievances, because they do not want to lose their jobs." As Williams states, Washington's warnings apply aptly to people like Jackson and Mfume.

Continuing, Robert Woodson, director of the Washington-based National Center for Neighborhood Enterprises, points to the increasing gap between the concerns of the civil rights establishment and those of ordinary black citizens for whom they to purport to speak in his book, "The Triumphs of Joseph."

One survey had 83% of blacks in favor of school choice, while in a floor vote at the 1993 NAACP convention, delegates passed a resolution opposing school choice. A Washington Post survey asked whether minorities should receive preferential treatment to make up for past discrimination-77% of black leaders said yes, while 77% of the black public said no. Black leaders support forced school busing, while a majority of blacks disapprove. Only eight percent of blacks said racial integration was an issue of importance, while the civil rights establishment continues their pursuit of 60's inspired agenda of mandated integration.

Perhaps, blacks, A-A's should look for leadership in the voice of former Oklahoma congressman J.C. Watts, who perhaps most accurately labeled the "Reverend" Jackson as a "poverty hustling pimp." Watts, quarterback at Oklahoma during my employment there, stresses the necessity of improving the black race through the family. If the parents are leading by example, then why are the blacks continuing to lag behind in school and prisons continue to fill up with a disproportionate percentage of their race?

"Racial profiling" is the latest term used as an attempt to cry racism and not face the reality of the problems. The facts are these: Blacks make up 12% of the population, but they have 56% of the arrests for murder, 42% for rape, 61% for robbery, 40% for car theft, and 39% for aggravated assault. The increase in African-American incarceration over the last decade is 800%. In perhaps the most honest statement of his career, the "Reverend" Jackson said "there is nothing more painful for me at this stage of my life than to walk down the street and hear footsteps and start thinking about robbery-then look around and see somebody white and feel relieved."

The problems for blacks do start with the family, but genetics could also be a factor. Indeed, testing conducted on different continents over a century shows strong evidence for racial variations in IQ. Whites have an average IQ of about 100, while Africans and African-Americans average from 70 to 85, and Asians from 106 to 113. Because of the continued pattern of a non-productive family legacy, blacks continue to fight an uphill battle. What can help? Neighborhood schools are beginning to crop up in black communities, finally with the support from the forward thinkers who know that education is the way to success. This can allow members of all races to make greater progress, but again the Hispanics influx is a tremendous negative. Our most populated state, California, struggles with the lack of English proficiency, having to hire numerous bilingual teachers. This is a problem spreading to other parts of the U.S., and bloated school system budgets with too many administrators and their school boards will likely attempt to solve the influx issue by increasing taxes. Is this the answer? No, it is time for the greed of lower pay and short-term higher company profits to be offset by stronger border enforcement. This situation can best be described like the old Fram oil filter commercial, "You can pay me now, or pay me later."

It also highlights the continued pattern of the Democrat Party to maintain a sense of beholding for those somewhat dependent on the government, either through employment or via government assistance. We begin with Franklin Roosevelt. The mainstream media has depicted him as a bold and decisive leader, who saved America from the ravages of depression and the advances of Nazi Germany. Read "The Media Sucks" chapter for more details, but this is another prime example of a whitewash. Let me give you five reasons, courtesy of "The Roosevelt Myth," by John T. Flynn. 1. The banking crisis could have been slowed and have aided in reducing the devastating effects of the depression. Roosevelt brushed off President Hoover's desperate pleas to support a plan to keep more banks from folding. The lame-duck President needed support, but Roosevelt "wished for the public to see his predecessor go out in a scene of utter ruin, setting the stage for him to be the savior to rebuild from the very bottom." 2. Seven years of raising taxes, creating agencies, incurring debt and punishing economic royalists did little to drop the unemployment rate and the nation remained in deep depression. He had little idea of how to fix the problems, relying on New Deal social tinkerers, whose notion was that the economy should be centrally planned and deep government spending was a good thing for the nation. 3. The WPA-still revered by most of the media-Works Progress Administration was adjunct to the Democratic election machine. Congressional testimony showed the needy were required to pledge portions of their salaries to the local party boss, and worked to re-elect Roosevelt and other Democrats to keep their checks coming. 4. Roosevelt campaigned against the ethics of crooked politics and promised an administration of the highest public standards (Impeached Bill Clinton did the same thing), Roosevelt's sons parlayed the Presidency into significant fortunes. They used the veiled threat of regulation to steer consulting, advertising and insurance (appropriate choice for crooks) business their way.

5. Roosevelt insisted on running for a fourth term, even though he could hardly function four hours a day. His post-World War II preparation was weak, allowing Stalin every whim under the illusion that the ruthless dictator would change his ways once Russia was part of a world organization.

The lasting legacy of Roosevelt, according to Flynn, is that he "replaced the traditional American system with something that finds Americans trapped in the economic disasters and political quarrels of every nation on Earth and a system of permanent militarism closely resembling that we beheld with horror in Europe for decades, with bureaucrats swarming over every field of life and the President calling for more power, more price-fixing, more regulation, and more billions." From the WPA plan during WWII for government jobs, there began a period of non-stop government growth and assistance, accelerated by the "Great Society" concept put forth by Lyndon Johnson, perhaps the President who did the most damage to the United States. Robert Caro, author of "Means of Ascent", a biography about Johnson, presented him as a boorish egomaniac willing to do anything-steal an election, lie about his war record, even risk his life-to advance himself. Johnson also frequently humiliated his wife and had a lengthy extramarital affair. According to Caro, "Johnson was all but totally consumed by his need for power and by his efforts to obtain it." Michael Kelly wrote of Johnson, "In his ferocity of ambition of duplicity, appetites, brutality, egomania, LBJ set the gold standard for monster hood. He was a thief of votes, and an acceptor of bribes, the hundred-dollar stuffed envelope had for him the comfort of a pocket-handkerchief. He betrayed anyone and everyone as he saw fit, from spouse to friend to Senate colleagues." Johnson bought and stuffed ballots on his way to the vice-presidency and then assumed the presidency after the assassination of John Kennedy. Why was Kennedy shot? Cubans, the Mafia, and our own government are suspects, but what about the fact that Kennedy was killed just three days after he had discussed dumping Johnson from the 1964 ticket and replacing him with former North Carolina governor, Terry Sanford? It is hard to steal an election without a payback required. Johnson would unleash his "Great Society" in 1965, starting the combined "guns and butter" concept that would morally and fiscally bankrupt the country. Despite the "Great Society" spending from $6-9 trillion on programs aimed at ending poverty, it mostly encouraged minorities to become dependent on government assistance, slowing robbing millions of families and individuals of their dignity and opportunity for success through their own efforts. But, there was a reason for this "enslavement" and it was to keep these people obligated for their vote. The greatest economic gains that black Americans made were from the end of World War II to about the mid 60's. Taxpayers foot the bill to prolong the agony for minorities and others and keep them from having the chance to develop their esteem and well being. This has prolonged the race division between blacks and whites, the division between rich and poor, and maintained a cycle of despair and dependency.

The cycle starts at birth. The worst examples are highlighted in our birth rates. Seventy percent, seven out of every ten blacks, are born without married parents. Our new nemesis, the Hispanics, are at 43%. Statistics show these numbers are extremely likely to continue the cycle of poor education, government dependence, and the creation of more babies without married parents. The initial welfare programs were bad enough, but the Aid for Dependent Children (ADC) program ignited the cycle in the 70's and 80's. Fortunately, the Republican Party started laying waste to ADC to try and slow this trend. It has been amazing to see how jobs were filled as the welfare rolls disappeared due to the new law eliminating benefits after two years. The overall U.S. rate was cut in half, while states like Wisconsin, Wyoming, and Idaho all had reduction rates of 80% and better. When talk started about the two-year time limit of welfare that was imposed, opponents predicted a grim future of hungry children and a swelling of homeless population. "Cruel and unusual punishment" is the way many critics of welfare reform described the effort to move welfare recipients off government assistance and into the workplace. The real cruel and unusual punishment is the old welfare system so dear to the hearts of those blind to its faults. The system amounted to no more than poverty-perpetuating bondage. The remedy for cruel and unusual is to help people learn a skill and get off welfare, period. Many states had tremendous amounts of money left over from their contingency funds that were to cushion the loss for those unable to get work. The welfare elimination bill was the law that Clinton signed, despite loud cries from the loser side of the Democrat Party. Fortunately, our hard-earned dollars are now being directed to more worthwhile necessities and the new workers can develop their lives and build self-esteem. It is scary to think how much earlier our balanced budget would have come without the near complete waste of taxpayer money.

Think of the legacy we have been left by the "Great Society." Many more children than necessary living a life of poverty and despair, plus the entrenched legacy of problems brought by the disincentives of welfare and ADC. But, it did help buy votes. Think of the Democrat Presidents since 1960. Kennedy, who may have stolen the election (Cook County in Illinois) and then paid a heavy price for the Bay of Pigs fiasco in Cuba, at least seemed to instill some confidence in America. Being a martyr does enhance the historical perspective, with Kennedy and John Lennon being prime examples. This leads us back to Johnson. "Landslide Lyndon", the nickname for an alleged ballot stuffed squeaker of an initial congressional victory, cost the country numerous young lives in Vietnam, spent the country into a spiral of wasteful spending during prosperous times, and began the cynical distrust of government. Well-earned, I might add. Who else could have lost the huge majority of 1964, the country wasn't quite ready for Goldwater, by not even being able to run in 1968? Johnson withdrew from the race and then hoped to be drafted as the nominee. Reports also indicate that the North Vietnamese were on the verge of surrender. Could Lyndon have been any worse? Finally, with the Republican Senate and Congress in place by 1994, the disastrous policies in place for nearly 30 years (maintained by Democrat majorities) have been scaled back considerably. I hope these changes will allow many of the less fortunate to establish self-esteem and find success in their business and personal lives.

Jimmy Carter was more than overmatched as President and it showed when Reagan trounced him in the 1980 election. I do admire Carter's post-presidency work with the Habitat for Humanity, but do not feel the same about his meddling in foreign matters or his violation of the unspoken rule not to criticize the sitting President.

Speaking of former Presidents, George Bush Sr. made two huge mistakes. The troops should have stayed in Iraq until they got Saddam. The argument against this idea was that we did not know who would have followed Saddam. Who could have been worse? While Bush made the bad decision on Saddam, after a brilliant war strategy, his most significant mistake was not presenting a bold economic plan immediately after the war. The window was there and the plan would have passed easily, guaranteeing an easy Bush win in '92. Since it appeared that George did not want to run anyway, this plan certainly would have made the campaign infinitely more palatable. The decision to reverse his stand on raising taxes was a significant blow to him, but he did have the economy on the rebound before he left office. Clinton did his best to take economy credit in his two terms, but the only credit he deserves is leaving well enough alone and allowing our technologically-advanced businesses lead the way in the world. I'll leave the rest of my wrath for Clinton in a later chapter.

Here are a few of my conclusions. If blacks would denounce the policies and actions of "Reverend" Jackson and others like him, then real and broad progress could be made in race relations and in the economic plight of blacks. Obviously, Jackson is no role model, having an affair with an employee and paying her out of Rainbow Coalition funds. Where was the IRS when you needed them? The emphasis should be on education; opening up opportunities for blacks that can be earned and appreciated. Discipline needs to be strictly enforced in the schools and perhaps even more so in the home.

Bill Cosby has been one of the few black celebrities to speak out against the hip-hop culture. A USA Today editorial read "Fortunately, there's one voice so clear and brilliant that it adds up to chorus. That voice belongs to comedian and activist Bill Cosby." Here is a portion of his speech to the NAACP convention on May 17, 2004. "Poor people-The lower economic and lower middle economic people are not holding up their end in this deal. In the neighborhood that most of us grew up in, parenting is not going on....I'm talking about people who cry when their son is standing there in an orange suit. Where were you when he was 2?

Where were you when he was 12? And where were you when he was 18, and how come you don't know he had a pistol?

I can't even talk the way these people talk. "Why you ain't where you is?" Everybody knows how important it is to speak English except those knuckleheads. You can't land a plane with "why you ain't." You can't be a doctor with that crap coming out of your mouth."

Answering his critics, Cosby said "A lot of the people who criticize me are angry because the job they were supposed to be doing hasn't been getting done."

The "Reverend" Jackson pays lip service to the "personal responsibility" mantra that Cosby espouses. As Greg Charles writes for USA Today, "Cosby is a much needed voice of reason for black Americans. Many so-called black leaders would rather cajole, incite or fleece institutions such as Wall Street firms into "paying up" for perceived racism. Jackson and others of his ilk, such as Al Sharpton and Louis Farrakan, should step aside and let someone with integrity take the reins. Black America is in deep trouble because of failed leadership."

The great Walter Williams gave this straightforward advice to young blacks: "I think a better message for avoiding poverty and incarceration is: Graduate from high school, get married before you have children and stay married. Work at any kind of job, even one that starts out paying minimum wage. Finally, do not engage in criminal behavior."

LETTERS FROM AMERICA

"I, too, am outraged and dumbfounded at how some of this country's black leaders pander to the continued picture of blacks as victims and rarely balance that by holding the young black male rappers and entertainers accountable for their misogynistic lyrics.

I have an eighteen year old son who embraced hip-hop rap music in his early teens, accepting without questions its hateful, destructive and misogynistic lyrics. Now, we have a generation of young blacks and whites who imitate the crass, degrading, and humiliating language and demeanor of stars who abandon any higher standard of intellect or behavior. My husband, our extended family and I cried "foul" loudly to our son. We printed off pages of lyrics and sat in front of him while he read them aloud. He, too, was stunned at the message being sent. Piles of CD's went into the trash, and he was held accountable for his choices from then on.

The leadership of this great country, parents being paramount, must assert its moral authority and continue the honest day to day work that will help bring all young people to the table of opportunity and equality. The lowest common denominator robs each of us of the God-given dignity that is our birthright."

KATHLEEN GORMAN RICE-Paradise Valley, AZ

CHAPTER FOUR

THE NEW (?) ENERGY CRISIS

I AM OLD ENOUGH to remember the "oil crisis" of the mid 1970's, having to purchase gas on the "even and odd" system. The last digit on your license plate determined whether you were "eligible" to purchase gas on a particular day. Gas prices skyrocketed as the Arab oil producers (now OPEC), hit the U.S. economy head-on, and inflation related to oil products crippled the economy in numerous ways.

While the price hike damaged business for a number of years, I believe there were other significant results of the crisis. A generation of greed was unleashed, as many people saw the extortion of the Arabs as a lesson in how to get ahead, ignoring the carnage that may be created in the pursuit.

Unfortunately, the desire for greed and power, in some cases, has not ebbed. Our past president and his N.Y. senator wife are perfect examples. A second consequence of the Arab grab was the breakdown of the traditional family-aided by the Great Society. With runaway inflation eating into buying power, many wives that were previously at home had no choice but to enter the job market. While I am not making any judgments on which spouse should be the "breadwinner," if a choice has to be made, it was a fundamental change in American society. Do I have any specifics to support these "theories?" No, I don't need them. The proof is out there. Kids are less disciplined, divorce rates are high, and we are a much less civil society. By the way, if I was a parent in the 70's, I would have liked to have been the stay-home Dad.

Now that I have given you a few ideas to ponder, let's move on to today's crisis. Attention to the situation began anew the summer of 2000, when gas prices spiked to $2.50 per gallon in California and some states in the Midwest. The formulation of some of the gas was blamed in the Midwest, as certain areas were forced by the government to use a different mixture of fuel.

The energy "shortage" continued into the winter of 2000, as natural gas prices soared to new heights, doubling and tripling the bills for many U.S. consumers. Those in the cold Northeast were especially affected.

Warmer weather brought some relief, but there were dire predictions of summer bringing even higher gasoline prices.

California continued to struggle with the electricity shortage that it created with an ill designed "deregulation" of its electricity industry. The problem was that retail prices were frozen, as then Governor Gray Davis tried to defy the laws of supply and demand. The cause of the "shortage" was simple. There was a booming economy and limited power-plant construction led to a scarcity of generating capacity. The capacity problem was compounded by lower levels of water, which are needed to produce hydroelectric power.

Major utilities were forced to sell many generating plants, as prices were initially lower. Purchases were made on the wholesale market, mainly, though not exclusively from companies that had purchased their old plants. The idea was that competition among power producers would keep wholesale prices low. When demand exceeded supply, Governor "Grayout" Davis resolutely refused to raise retail rates. The top two utilities, Pacific Gas and Electric and Southern California Edison, became insolvent.

Governor Davis, looking to blame someone else for the crisis, tried to bail out the two utilities that gave $500,000 to his campaign fund. The companies also employed some of Davis' top political advisors, who also worked for state government.

Forced to conserve or face additional blackouts, Californians cut back their electricity use and the summer of 2001 passed without serious difficulties. Many lessons can be taken from the situation in California. First of all, what was the biggest cause of the shortage? I would say a tie between the ultimate self-serving plan of Governor Davis and his puppets, and the reasons stated by Phyllis Schlafy. "Isn't California's energy crisis really because of the large increase in its illegal population during a decade when no new power plants were built? California now has about four million illegal aliens, so it's no wonder that existing sources of power are not adequate."

China and India are now causing a significant run up in the cost of oil; as their economies play catch up for years of neglect or oppressive government rule. Personally, I think Saudi Arabia and Kuwait owe us for the Gulf War and ridding the region of Saddam. This should come in the form of more stable oil prices, but that is not occurring. However, this should also be a two-way street. As was shown during the Gray Davis electricity crisis, it is possible to survive reductions in electricity use without sacrificing our lifestyle. Due to drought and population increases, many areas of the country are discovering this is true with water as well, but this will be discussed later. There needs to be additional effort to be as energy efficient as possible without affecting business production or reducing individual comfort. I like it cool in my house! Additionally, we have to vigorously pursue other sources of energy. First on my list is wind power, catching hold in the Southwest and Midwest as a significant power producer. Next is the Alaska National Wildlife Refuge (ANWR). Largely barren and deeply frozen a large portion of the year, ANWR holds substantial promise with significant oil and natural gas reserves.

Estimates are four billion barrels of oil, enough to provide seven years of consumption at 2004 levels. Energy producers and environmental extremists need to work together for the good of the country on ANWR and get it done soon. The area under consideration is only 2,000 acres. Significant technology advances in drilling techniques can limit the disruption of ANWR and help us reduce our dependence on OPEC. Offshore drilling and oil shale also need to be approved.

Now that the environmentalists are pissed off, let me raise their temperatures a bit more. Global warming is not, in the words of stiff Al Gore, a "planetary emergency." In July of 2001, there was an article in "Consumers Research" titled: Global Warming: Fact or Fiction. A 3,000-page report had MIT professor Richard Lindzen as the lead author. Here are the conclusions: "Our primary conclusion was that despite some knowledge and agreement, the science is by no means settled. We are quite confident that the global mean temperature is about 0.5 degrees Celsius higher than a century ago. We are not in a position to confidently attribute past climate change to carbon dioxide or to forecast what the climate change will be in the future."

Fred Singer, President of the Science and Environmental Project in Arlington, VA says they used four independent data sets for measuring the warming. Weather stations around the world showed warming over the last 30 years, but not in the United States. Weather satellites and weather balloons showed no warming. Proxy data, consisting of tree rings, ice cores, lake sediments, etc. also showed no warming.

In the mid 1970's, the extremists were predicting an ice age with wholesale death and misery for mankind. The extremists and Democrats need to stop demonizing this issue for the sake of the country's energy necessities. The Democrats also try scaring minorities, gays, seniors and the afflicted in every campaign. A better-educated and aware public would completely reject these tactics.

With the price of oil reaching $100, the oil dependent economies of the world are facing potential disaster. Gas prices in the U.S. approached four dollars a gallon, even as the heavy driving season is upon us. The high prices are funding the governments of a number of countries working against the United States. Phil Verleger, one of the U.S. top energy consultants, said "U.S. energy policy today is in support of terrorism-not the war on terrorism."

Seven state-owned national companies now control almost one-third of the oil products and reserves. Those seven are Saudi Arabia-Aramco, Russia-Gazprom, China-CNPC, Iran-NIOC, Venezuela-PDVSA, Brazil-Petrobras, and Malaysia-Petronas. In addition to significant control of the market, these countries are not investing as much in product and investment, not wanting to risk investing in new capacity that might cause a price decline. As Tom Friedman put it, "Oil regimes do not have to modernize or govern well. They just buy off their people and their mullahs."

While the search for additional oil sources will not solve the long-term energy crisis, as noted by U.S. News editor Mortimer Zuckerman, "some trade-off is going to have to be considered, and this will roil the political scene forever." The continental shelf in the United States is estimated to have enough oil for 116 million cars for 47 years. The Energy Department and private industry estimates there are a trillion barrels of oil in Colorado, and possibly twice that in the entire Green River Formation, which includes eastern Utah and southwest Wyoming. Much of this oil will have to be extracted as oil shale, a process that is more expensive, harder on the environment, and uses substantial water, two to five barrels of water per barrel of oil. Water is another issue where serious long-range planning is required.

In addition to oil shale, nuclear energy must be utilized. Seventy-five percent of France's electrical power is provided by nuclear energy. At present, 103 nuclear plants generate about 20% of the U.S. electricity. There has only been one U.S. nuclear accident, with no fatalities. One person has an open mind about it. Patrick Moore, who helped start the environmental group Greenpeace, said "I now believe we environmentalists need to take a fresh look at nuclear energy, which just may be the energy source that can save our planet."

The full-scale approach to moving away from oil should also contain wind, solar, hydrogen, diesel, and ethanol. Solar is becoming economically feasible, rooftop panels averaging around $30,000 per home. Fourteen states are offering cash rebates, dropping the out of pocket cost by more than half in some cases. The average savings from the panels has reached $1,500 per year, providing a payback in less than ten years. In Nevada, the Solar One power plant is now generating 64 megawatts of electricity, enough for 40,000 homes. The plant uses acres of mirrors to harness solar radiation to drive a turbine. In 2006, thousands of homes and businesses such as Staples, Whole Foods, and Wal-Mart installed 120 megawatts of new solar capacity, up 600% since 2000. Germany has gone much further, creating a national plan and installing ten times the U.S. capacity in 2006. One million homes now use the solar power and the plan has helped create 170,000 jobs for solar manufacturing companies.

Wind is the fastest growing renewable energy. A wind turbine is being built every four hours, but, at present, this technology is providing less than one percent of our nation's electricity. The push is on for larger scale wind power, such as the Britannia Project in England, a research program to produce the world's largest off-shore wind turbine. The 7.5-megawatt mammoth turbine would have a 492 foot diameter rotor, 50 percent wider and provide more than double the output of the company manufacturer Clipper's current largest model, Offshore. It would be able to take advantage of higher, steadier wind and proximity to population centers.

In the U.S., the focus is more on shore, in the center of the country, especially Texas. The cost of wind power is just eight cents per kilo-watt hour unsubsidized, compared to the average electricity price of 10.5 cents.

Hydrogen powered cars, which use hydrogen and oxygen to create a reaction that produces electricity, but emit only water vapor, have already shown up in Florida, New York, and California. The extensive use of natural gas in the process could make it less attractive, in addition to the fact that the hydrogen refueling stations will have to be constructed. State and private funds are being combined to build as many as 200 stations by 2010. General Motors says it hopes to begin pumping hundreds of hydrogen fuel-cell vehicles a year into public hands through GM dealerships by 2011. GM is "working as hard and fast as we can for competitive reasons" said Larry Burns, GM VP Research and Development. Hydrogen is highly volatile, making storage a serious issue.

Diesel, and the paths to it, may present one of the better options. Chicken fat and cottonseed oil can be mixed with soybean oil to produce bio-diesel. Tyson Chicken has already established a renewable energy division, and Perdue and Smithfield Foods are doing the same. Vernon Edelman, Professor of Economics at Minnesota, has done extensive study of bio-diesel and estimates that within five years that the U.S. will produce one billion gallons of bio-diesel, half of it from animal fat, presently selling for 19 cents a pound. Soybean oil, which is presently about 90% of bio-diesel, could then be reduced to about 20%. The soybean oil is needed to add necessary lubrication for the engine parts. Edelman states that animal fat is the key to making bio-diesel a reliable fuel for U.S. trucking fleets. Plants are popping up across the country, led by South Carolina, Missouri, North Carolina and Texas. Tyson alone could produce 300 million gallons of fat to convert to fuel. Production of bio-diesel doubled from 2005 to 2006, 75 to 150 million gallons, and was expected to double again in 2007. Federal tax breaks are helping to make diesel a competitive fuel.

Ethanol has received significant attention, but I believe there have been some mistakes made in this direction. Corn has been the main focus in producing the ethanol, but while helping to make the fuel, it has created problems. The energy used is more than what is produced, and the heavy use of corn has caused significant food inflation. Balance is needed here, and a heavier focus on the pursuit of "cellulosic ethanol." This fuel is made by breaking down the tough starches found in hardier plant matter-from cornstalks to fast-growing switch grass to paper-mill waste. Work is needed to make it economic, mainly through bioengineering. The government estimates the first cellulosic plant will cost five times that of a corn refinery and not able to begin operation until 2010.

Private business thinks otherwise. Range Fuels, a Colorado firm founded by venture capitalist Vinod Khosia, is aiming to beat the government date by two years. Located near Georgia forestland, the company plans to refine abundant timber-industry waste wood, and bypass the use of expensive enzymes. Instead, they will use heat and pressure to convert wood chips to gas, then extract ethanol with a catalyst. The process is a modern version of the proven Fischer-Tropsch process developed in Germany in the 1920's to make diesel fuel from coal.

Brazil has made great strides using ethanol powered by sugar cane. Seventy percent of new cars are using the fuel, and it has become a thriving free market business. Ethanol pumps are at every filling station, and there is plentiful land available for more sugar cane. The cost of production is $1.10 per gallon.

Sugar cane waste is burned to generate steam for turbines, meeting all of the ethanol plant's electricity needs. Excess power will soon light up half of the homes in Sao Tome, a southern Brazil town of 6,000.

Other technologies gaining favor are the harnessing of waves for energy, where the Federal Energy Regulatory Commission has cleared 21 preliminary projects with 35 pending. Water is 850 times more dense than air, allowing tidal turbines to produce 40 times more power than windmills with similar gear. The highly predictable tidal flows can be detected several years in advance.

Lithium batteries are showing great promise in powering the new hybrid cars. Mercedes and Nissan are making great strides in this direction. Geothermal power is also very promising , and the U.S. is the world's biggest mass producer of it.

This is a battle that has to be won. We are really fighting again for our independence. Cal Thomas has a great slogan for our "Energy Independence Day-Let 'Em Eat Sand".

BE SMART ABOUT THE CHOICES

According to a new-cost benefit analysis of alternative fuels by researcher John Graham at the Pardee Rand Graduate School, anything's better than ethanol blend E85, even ordinary gasoline.

Diesel scored highest, surprising even the researchers. "We were kind of expecting that hybrids would outperform diesels when we went into the study. It's close, but the advanced diesel provides better performance and fuel economy for the price" said Graham.

Compared to gasoline, a driver could spend as much as $1,600 more on fuel over a vehicle's life burning E85, a mix of 85% ethanol and 15% gasoline, Graham calculates, while a diesel could save as much as $2300. Diesels are just coming back into the USA as automakers introduce clean-burning models that meet new pollution rules.

Do we jump from E10 (10% ethanol) to E85? "That's not a logical leap. That's why we're looking at these intermediate blends," says Brian Jennings, Executive Vice-President at the American Council for Ethanol. Graham's team calculated the individual and societal costs and benefits of conventional gasoline vehicles, gasoline-electric hybrids, high-tech diesels and flex-fuel vehicles burning E85 full time. The conclusion was that unless gas prices, averaging $3.10 per gallon at the time, rise above $4 and average $3.50

the next few years, or ethanol prices drop a lot, diesel's the best overall solution and E85 is the worst.

Ethanol has less than 70% of the energy of gasoline, so more ethanol in the blend means fewer miles per gallon. Adjusted for lower energy content, E85 averaged about $3.25, AAA reported Thursday, November 29, 2007. Drawbacks outweigh the high marks ethanol gets for adding almost nothing to the cost of a vehicle modified to burn E85 for energy independence, Graham's team concluded.

MORE GREED

High gas prices piss me off. But, greed is playing even more of a role than previously. Reading from various sources, I have found that it is estimated that anywhere from $20-50 of the price of a barrel of oil is created by those speculating in the commodity. This means up to 50% of the price of gas is due to speculators. Is this necessary?

LETTERS FROM AMERICA

I seem to remember that when the first oil crunch occurred back in the 1970's, the oil companies said that, along with the crude oil still in the ground, there was a huge amount of oil shale, just lying around, waiting to be used.

The only problem was that until gasoline went to $1.75 per gallon, it was not economical to process it. Gasoline at that time was around $1 per gallon. Well, its 30-some years later, and gasoline topped $1.75 per gallon a long time ago.

I guess that I'm not very observant, because I cannot seem to find any newspaper articles or TV reports concerning the progress of bringing this refined shale oil to market. What is the holdup, I wonder? Is this just a ploy to keep prices up so oil companies can rape the public longer?

Oh wait. It just struck me. They are saving it for when, due to political pressure from all the other countries, no other oil producing countries will sell us any crude oil, as we will be shunned by them. Maybe our government does know something that we don't.

ART STEIN-Bradenton, FL

CHAPTER FIVE

PORK BARREL GOVERNMENT AND BUYING YOUR VOTE

THIS IS MY last chapter, at least in the order that I wrote them. Government is not my favorite subject, although it will receive a proportional amount of my wrath.

A report was prepared for Congress' Joint Economic Committee, titled "The Size and Function of Government and Economic Growth." The report was by James Gwartney and Randall Holcombe, economics professors at Capital University in Columbus, Ohio. At the time of the report, the good news was that the expansion of the U.S. economy had moved into its eighth year and it had been fifteen years since a major recession. Despite the expansion, the real rate of economic growth during the 1990's was less than half that achieved in the 1960's. The fact is that our average rate of growth had fallen during each of three decades.

Greater economic stability, but less rapid growth, has also been the pattern of other developed nations. The report, using data from 60 nations, produces convincing evidence that there's a strong negative relationship between the size of government, increases in government expenditures, and economic growth.

In the United States, the authors conclude: If government expenditures, as a percent of gross domestic product (GDP) had remained at their 1960 level, the 1996 GDP would have been $9.16 trillion instead of $7.64 trillion. That translates into $23,440 in additional income for the average family of four. Those "Great Society" expenditures robbed all of us, and what did they accomplish? They made the U.S. poorer financially and spiritually.

The authors also compared developed countries with the smallest increases in the size of government between 1960 and 1996 to those with the largest increases and looked at their growth rates. In 1960, government spending as a percentage of GDP in the United States, Iceland, Ireland, United Kingdom and New Zealand averaged 28.9%. The growth rate for those countries averaged 4.3%. In 1996, government spending in those countries had risen to an average of 39.1%, and their growth rates fell, averaging 2.7%.

Developed nations with the largest increases in government size between 1960 and 1996 were Portugal, Spain, Greece, Finland,

Sweden and Denmark. In 1960, those governments spent an average of 28.1% of their GDP, and their growth rates averaged 6.4%. In 1996, government spending averaged 54.5% of GDP, and their growth rates fell to an average of 1.2%.

From the statistical estimates, the professors show that for each 10% in growth in government spending, there is a 1% decrease in growth. As governments move beyond their core functions, they adversely affect economic growth through the disincentive effects of taxation, diminishing returns as government takes on activities for which it is ill suited and government interference with the wealth-creation process. Governments aren't as effective as markets in adjusting to changing circumstances and distances innovative production methods.

Washington, wake up and cut out the waste. Voters, wake up and vote out those who waste. Does the $23,440 loss of income help you get the message?

Who made it worse? The Perjurer-in-Chief, Bill Clinton, insisted upon restoring food stamp benefits for about 250,000 illegal immigrants in an attachment aimed at helping farmers. The 1996 welfare overhaul bill had cut these immigrants off welfare. This was $818 million of benefits. As Senator Phil Gramm stated, "the biggest problem with this bill is it puts a great big neon sign at the border of the United States of America, Come and get welfare." I guess a lot of illegals saw the sign.

Haven't these government programs failed often enough for people to know they are going to get fleeced again? Apparently not, or as Walter Williams would put it, "Ignorance gives politicians a free hand to exploit the politics of envy."

More of the cold hard facts on how bad the bureaucracy is doing its job. An estimated 30 cents on the dollar is lost to overhead. Remember the $640 toilet seat of the 1980's? It was replaced by the $76 screw, normally costing 57 cents. According to an analysis by the Heritage Foundation, the federal education bureaucracy runs more than 788 programs in 40 different agencies at a cost of nearly $100 billion annually. Obviously, we are not getting our money's worth in federal education spending as the performance of our public schools continues to decline. The programs to address problems with juveniles stretch over ten departments, three independent agencies, one federal commission, one presidential council and one quasi-official agency. The 131 juvenile programs cost over $4 billion annually. Twenty billion dollars a year is spread over 15 different federal agencies for job training.

Seventy programs in 57 agencies to fight illegal drug use cost taxpayers $16 billion a year. The Government Accounting Office has stated that most federal agencies cannot determine the effectiveness of their programs. Note-these numbers were before the Bush presidency.

The trends are bad, as politicians continue to protect business, the unions, and the many "squeaky wheel" groups that lobby the Congress and the Senate. Professors James Buchanan and Gordon Tullock of George Mason University call it "rent seeking", or the use of government as a means to acquire greater wealth by gaining monopoly power or income transfers. U.S. automakers and unions have gotten Congress to enact quotas and tariffs on foreign imports. Dairymen and sugar producers want import restrictions on their products, while labor unions want minimum wage-law and other legislation to help eliminate competition. Import restrictions on Japanese cars during the 1980's cost U.S. car buyers about $4.3 billion, or approximately $160,000 per year for each job saved in Detroit. It certainly would have been cheaper to allow imports and give laid-off workers $60,000 a year and a start on other job training. Most of you reading this book probably work hard to make a living, and the government is taking your money and wasting it-pure and simple.

Sticking to his campaign promise to cut income taxes, President George W. Bush quoted Democrat President John Kennedy, who proposed cutting taxes 45 years ago. Kennedy said "The greatest danger is a tax cut too little or too late to be effective." The tax cut was "for those in the lower income brackets who are certain to spend their additional home pay, and for those in the middle and upper income brackets, who can thereby be encouraged to undertake additional efforts to invest more capital."

Three times, across-the-board rate cuts have grown the U.S. economy, raised tax revenues and lowered the percentage of the tax burden for lower income earners. In 1981, Ronald Reagan's across-the-board tax cuts accelerated the recovery from 13.5% inflation, 7.5% unemployment and a prime rate of 21%. Democrats complain that the deficits increased under Reagan, but they forget to tell you that Federal Reserve Chairman Paul Volcker squeezed credit, causing a recession and wiping out revenue projections. There was increased defense spending under Reagan, the result being that Russia collapsed trying to match the U.S. spending, and much of the tension of the "Cold War" was reduced.

Tired of worrying about taxes? At the time of my research for this chapter, the IRS reported that the average taxpayer spends over 27 hours a year on necessary record keeping. Tax instructions totaled 117 pages, triple that of 1975. The IRS was printing 943 forms and instructions, totaling 12,933 pages! Reviewing the most "serious problems" for taxpayers, the IRS reported that "tax complexity for individuals and businesses as number one and two" and the "root cause" of the top 20 problems.

Knowing when to quote those with greater intelligence, I repeat the words of 19th century philosopher-economist Frederic Bastiat, "The state is the great fiction by which everyone seeks to live at the expense of everyone else." Hey Freddie, an excellent observation.

Here is another one-"the shift from personal autonomy to dependence on government is perhaps the defining characteristic of modern American politics. In the span of barely one lifetime, a nation grounded in ideals of individual liberty has been transformed into one in which federal decisions control even such personal matters as what health care we buy-a nation now so bound up in detailed laws and regulation that no one can know what all the rules are: let alone comply with them."-Professor Charlotte Twight from her book, "Dependent on DC."

There are other inefficient aspects of government that are even more obvious. The first is road construction. This one has affected me directly over the last two years. A three mile road project that was scheduled to be completed in less than two years will now be finished in over three years. The delay has caused a number of the businesses along the three mile stretch to suffer significant financial loss. State government blames local government, local government blames contractors, contractors blame sub-contractors, utility companies get blamed; pretty much the same story every time. When I was in Chapel Hill, a 12 mile stretch of road heading south was scheduled to start in March of 2001 and scheduled to be completed in December 2003, but was delayed to June of 2005.

How about the worst project? I am going with the "Big Dig" in Boston. The original estimate was $2.6 billion and eight years for completion. The final tally was $14.8 billion and 13 years. "The project never would have won the support of federal or state officials-or the public-if the true cost had been known in advance," said David Luberoff, co-author of "Mega-Projects", which looks at the politics of projects like the Big Dig. Even with the thirteen plus years, there have still been problems with the most expensive public works project in American history. In September 2004, more than 400 leaks were found in the tunnel, requiring the use of sandbags, closing lanes, and backing up traffic more than ten miles. The tunnel drain was expected to handle 500,000 gallons of water per year, but 26 million gallons flowed from December 2003 to September 2004. Blame? The project contractor and the Massachusetts Turnpike Authority apparently knew about the leak issue in 1999 and did nothing. The Authority blamed the construction manager, who points to a major contractor who says the authority knew about it.

All the years of road construction and these projects still take too long and cost too much. What is the constant factor? Government. They should be held accountable.

Another of my targets is the Food and Drug Administration (FDA). In a November 2004 hearing, the office of the FDA's office of drug safety testified about approved drugs that were causing serious side effects. Meredia, a weight loss pill, was causing high blood pressure. Crestor, a cholesterol drug, was linked to kidney failure, Bextra, a pill for arthritis, showed an increase in the incidence of stroke and heart attack, and Severent, a treatment for asthma, had side effects tied to pulmonary disease. There were even reports of patients found dead clutching their Severent inhaler.

Was the cause a decrease in enforcement? From 1996 to 2001, the FDA issued 480 cease and desist letters. The next four years there were 130, despite a steadily rising number of reports of potentially adverse side effects. Senator Charles Grassley of Iowa stated "The kind of mismanagement we've seen this year by the FDA demands tough scrutiny. One of my concerns is that the FDA has a relationship with drug companies that is too cozy and that's exactly the opposite of what it should be."

Perhaps the worst story is the approval of aspartame, also known as NutraSweet. I am horrified that the approval occurred during the administration of my favorite President, Ronald Reagan. Many of you may be surprised by the person who appeared to play the largest part in gaining approval; Donald Rumsfeld, who was hired as G.D. Searle's President in early 1977. According to a former G.D. Searle salesperson, Patty Wood-Allot , "Rummy" told the sales force that, if necessary, "he would call in all his markers and no matter what, he would see to it that aspartame would be approved that year (1981)." This is bad stuff. **Listen to me!!!!!** Stop using it now. **It is poison to your body.** Brain damage, uterine polyps, high blood pressure are just a start. There are numerous web sites highlighting the dangers of NutraSweet, including the Aspartame Toxicity Information Center. I could write a whole book on this subject, especially the scandalous approval process, but I'll limit it for now. Here is a concise look at the product: It appears to cause slow, silent damage in those unfortunate enough to not have immediate reactions and a reason to avoid it. It may take one year, five years, ten years, or 40 years, but it seems to cause some reversible and some irreversible changes in health over long-term use.

This is from a person labeled "An Aspartame Victim": "I know that the average consumer has a devil-may-care something-is-gonna-kill-me attitude...but they don't realize that before THIS stuff kills they are going to have a miserable declining existence with LOTS of pain and other problems (not to mention cancer, tumors, and maybe even Alzheimer's or similar things) before death solves the problem."

FDA Investigator and Toxicologist, Dr. Adrian Gross stated the following: "The cancer-causing potential of aspartame is a matter that has been established way beyond any reasonable doubt."

Damn, "Rummy", not enough troops in Iraq and you plague us with NutraSweet. You should be in my "Idols and Assholes" chapter.

LETTERS FROM AMERICANS

"How great for taxpayers to spend more of their own money to their choosing rather than by government politicians buying their re-election. It's time to reign in mostly unconstitutional big government by having a taxpayers' (tea party) rebellion against the federal and state government."

Fred Schmidt, Fearrington Village, NC

"The response of Sen. Barbara Boxer, D-Calif. to USA Today's editorial on pork in the recent water projects bill is one to expect from Congress ("Entirely justifiable projects, Opposing view, Flood control debate, Wednesday).

Rather than address the pork, she simply lists several meaningful projects in the bill—as if the existence of a few worthwhile projects indicates that all of the projects are worthwhile. What nonsense.

Why is that when Congress dips into the national treasury and takes money to buy favors and votes, it's considered politics as usual? Then, when CEO's, such as the ex-Tyco head Dennis Kozlowski, dip into their company's treasury to foot frivolous purchases, it's called a felony. I don't really see much difference between the two."

Charles M. Masson-New York

CHAPTER SIX

URBAN SPRAWL-
IT MAY BE COMING TO
YOUR TOWN

WHILE I WAS growing up, our family would take annual summer trips to Alabama to visit my mother's relatives. The trips became drudgery after the grueling 16 hour drive with a family of six. Even then, in the early to mid 60's, the trip was timed to avoid the afternoon traffic of Atlanta. Interstates were not as prevalent, which made the trip several hours longer than it would be today. I suppose, subconsciously, that this started my intense hate of traffic congestion.

My hometown of Chapel Hill did not have problems with congestion until the last decade or so. Now, the attraction of the college town with a moderate climate has drawn numerous retirees and others who have tried to escape their previous battles with congestion or miserable weather of the Northeast or upper Midwest. Most of my spotlight will be on Chapel Hill, although I will also visit many other parts of the U.S. In Chapel Hill, I saw a small college town, once called a village; have its landscape stampeded by a population explosion. Despite many lengthy discussions between developers, town councils, etc., the growth has already damaged much of the beauty of the area, increased traffic exponentially, sparked a growth in crime and become a magnet for the lower rungs of society.

In Chapel Hill, the growth has begun to diminish the beauty of the area. A local put it succinctly: "To me (and others I know), it seems more as if the town has been over-accommodating to the pressures and wishes of developers, commercial interests and the University. Our taxes continue to increase while the joy and benefits of being a town resident decrease. Chapel Hill is on the edge of its financial transformation into a congested and over-developed place, with too many students, too little social and economic diversity, and overwhelmed educational and municipal service systems." Thanks to Natalie Amarelle-then resident of Chapel Hill.

A writer for the "Chapel Hill Newspaper", Linda Haac, took a gaze into the future with an article. "Welcome to our fair city in the year of 2005, when the venerable old Southern village has transformed itself into the shape of, believe or not, New Jersey. Or, as some people around the country now refer to us: Los Angeles East." The article continues, "Taking any approach to our fair city and its eight lanes coming in (in some cases, 12, if you're lucky and don't want to sit in bumper-to-bumper traffic for hours) and more pavement coming every day. North Carolina used to be known as "the good roads state", but now, people joke about us being the "all-roads state." We used to have neighborhoods, but now we have satellite cities."

Continuing her article, Haac paints an extremely dim picture. "So when you wake up today, make sure you listen to the radio to hear the traffic report. Our zip code may be akin to that of Beverly Hills or Brentwood, but this is still L.A. East: massive traffic jams, smog-clogged air, heat from unrelenting stretches of pavement, helicopters zooming overhead, jet airplanes screaming in low and once or twice falling into schools, people wiping out on freeways: In short, a paradise trashed." Linda, I wish you were wrong, but you are not. Sam Nicholas, I agree with you when you said "the Town Council should preserve our community and develop it with great vision, and not rubber stamp poorly designed projects."

Unfortunately for North Carolina, the growth problem is not reserved for the Triangle area. Wilmington grew from 55,000 people in 1992 to nearly 95,000 by 2005. The main thoroughfares of Market Street, South College Road and Oleander Drive are already over capacity. The growth is spreading north of the city to Hampstead, severely overcrowding the schools and roads.

In Charlotte, NC, Mecklenburg County, growth has reduced the acres of trees from nearly 163 thousand acres in 1984 to fewer than 106 thousand by 2003, a drop of 35 percent. Atlanta and Seattle, among other cities, have seen similar loss of tree cover. More buildings mean more use of energy, warmer cities with the loss of tree cover, and the likely permanent loss of many beautiful areas.

While I was overexposed to the growth of "urban sprawl" in North Carolina, there are many parts of the country facing the same difficulties. A N.Y. Times article on this issue stated the following, "Although the causes of sprawl are complex, it is clear that population growth is central to it. High rates of immigrants, one million per year, and a high natural growth rate add two and a half million yearly to the U.S. population." Please note that the immigrant total is composed of "legal" immigrants only. This is part of a bigger problem addressed in chapter two. The article continues by noting that "these population growth rates will overwhelm even well-designed cities. Until our population policies are updated to reflect these new realities, efforts to engineer our way out of these problems will have limited results."

Nationwide, gridlock on the roads is creeping into some cities as early as five AM. More than ten percent of the nation's commuters now leave for work between five to six AM. The average driver now spends 443 hours yearly behind the wheel, or the equivalent of 11 work weeks.

Another argument of developers is that limiting growth will shoot up the cost of housing. A 1992 study of 14 California cities, half with strong growth controls and half with none, showed no difference in average housing prices.

The problems of urban sprawl are very widespread and need our immediate attention. It is not just limited to the largest cities. In Utah, a $10 billion highway was built through the majestic Wasatch Range. The road has sparked construction of more housing developments and ugly shopping strips, but more importantly it will destroy over half of the dairy farms near Salt Lake City. You and I paid for this destruction.

If you think you can escape the congestion by moving from a large city to a smaller one, I have to warn you that projections indicate the problems of sprawl are likely to hit smaller areas harder in the future. The estimates show that cities of 500,000 or less will experience a 150% growth in congestion, compared to an increase of 65% for cities of more than three million. According to projections, many mid-size communities like Sacramento, Charlotte, Tucson and Orlando will experience congestion worse than present day Chicago. Do we have to accept this "inevitable growth?" Not in the words of Sarasota County, FL commissioner Jon Thaxton. "Sarasota should strive to become an exemplary midsize city that recognizes open space, agriculture and environmentally sensitive areas as permanent uses, rather than lands in holding pattern for "inevitable growth" yet to come. Focus more on promoting economic, capital, social and spiritual growth than on population growth. Many communities with stable populations develop these other areas and provide a high-quality, attractive living environment for their citizens. A community that deliberately plans to preserve its unique character will prosper economically and distinguish itself from other areas that accepted the defeatist slogan of "inevitable growth" at any cost and overdeveloped themselves into oblivion."

Thaxton's philosophy is in tune with his constituents. In the November 2007 election, two Venice, FL commissioners and the mayor were soundly defeated by three "slow-growth" candidates. In addition, supermajority measures passed in the city and the county of Sarasota. These measures will make it much more difficult for new growth to be approved. As prominent local developer Henry Rodriguez saw it, "There is a general feeling of anger toward growth. They're just angry." The very large newspaper headline in the Herald-Tribune, the day after the vote, read **"ANGER TOWARD GROWTH."**

Many environmentalists and urban planners will want to solve the congestion by building mass transit. In the book, "The Road More Traveled": Why the Congestion Crisis Matters More than You Think, and What We Can do About It," Ted Balaker and Sam Staley argue against it, noting that mass transit workforce use is less than 5%. Their solution is to build more roads, evidenced by the fact that L.A. has the least amount of pavement per person and Dallas has the most, and half the congestion. To emphasize how growth has overwhelmed capacity, there are 70 million more people in the U.S. than 25 years ago and the total highway miles have increased just over five percent.

Balaker and Staley advocate the use of dynamic pricing, already being used on I-15 in southern California. Using a system called Fastrak, electronic signs post the cost of use of special access lanes, changing prices as often as every six minutes to help prevent congestion. A pocket size radio transmission device is in the transponder, paying from a pre-paid account. Carpoolers and mass transit users are not charged for the lane use. The book concludes that "New electronic technologies, harnessed to private capital and profit motive, can nimbly use price incentives to produce new traffic patterns and driving habits, thereby increasing America's freedom to pursue happiness, speedily." Like other large problems, bold action is needed to solve them, and we need to listen to people like Balaker and Staley.

I have highlighted the reasons of urban sprawl and it is way past time for action. A limit on and stronger controls on immigration, as well as an organized set of land-use planning policies for communities can help stop the bulldozers. We need urban planning, not government planning. The dirty secret of pro-sprawlers is that they can only do it with taxpayer money. The public, not the developers, pays for it. I want my hard-earned federal tax dollars to be used to judiciously manage future growth. If those who can make a difference in the future planning will do so, many areas can be saved from unmanaged growth. If not, many towns and cities will watch the quality and beauty of their areas disappear before their eyes…and you can't reverse the damage.

THE CALIFORNIA FIRES-2007

Due to the drought in Florida in 2007, there were wildfires in various parts of the state. One day the fires were close enough to fill the sky and obscure the beautiful Florida sun. Fortunately, there has been minimal residential damage in the state. California has not been so lucky. In late October, the fires hit the area from San Diego to the mountains north of Los Angeles. As of October 25th, the wildfires had consumed 1,500 homes, forced more than a half million people to evacuate and caused more than $1 billion worth of damage. Residents talked about the accelerated growth as a reason for the significant damage. "They've been chopping off mountains, clearing avocado groves, and they don't have roads for all the people" said Linda Harrison after she had fled her home north of San Diego.

People moving to those places "are putting themselves at increased risk" said Mark Rey, the Agriculture Department undersecretary who oversees the U.S. Forest Services. "This is something we've let develop, and we'll have to deal with the consequences of that."

Newcomers have built at least 16,000 homes in the fire zone since 2000. The population in those neighborhoods grew about 16% since 2000, double California's overall growth, according to Claritas, a marketing research firm.

CHAPTER SEVEN

IT SMELLS LIKE ASS OUT HERE

THIS WAS DEFINITELY not an original chapter idea, but I was inspired by two factors. A co-worker in the UNC Ticket Office provided me a copy of "George" magazine during the late 1990's, mainly because Ann Coulter had an article in it. After first reading Ann's article, I continued through the magazine until finding a story about the hog farm business. The story featured one of America's largest farm executives and the background of his rise in the swine industry. His great success was not the major focus of the story, however. With pigs, there is tremendous waste, and the problem of disposing of it. A large hog farm has a huge lagoon where the hog waste is deposited and basically "ferments" until it can be used as fertilizer or other similar purposes. Two serious problems exist with the process. While the waste is "fermenting", the stench can be stifling. While driving to the beach in North Carolina on Interstate 40, there is about a 50-mile stretch where you can get an unpleasant whiff of the odor. After the floods from Hurricane Floyd in 1999, that stretch was almost impassable due to the smell.

The smell reminds me of a "South Park" episode where Eric Cartman steps off a bus upon his arrival in Costa Rica, holds his nose, and proclaims that "it smells like ass out here." It is one of my favorite scenes from the classic animated series, accented by Eric's pronunciation of the word here, pronounced "hyuh." The scene gave me the chapter title idea.

As the article in "George" informs us, the crisis of hog waste disposal has already evolved. One serious incident occurred in 1995, when heavy rains helped swell several lagoons that overflowed into rivers, killing numerous fish and endangering the water supply of much of eastern North Carolina. In May, 1998, a 5,000 gallon spill occurred ten miles upstream from the Northeast Cape Fear River, and waste was detected two miles downstream. Earlier in April, a 1.9 million-gallon spill entered the swampy waters feeding the Northeast Cape Fear.

The problem is not isolated in North Carolina. In southern Utah, western Oklahoma and central Wisconsin, the hog-empire has also reared its ugly snout. But, perhaps, North Carolina has been affected the most. Statistics from the Southern Environmental Center showed that 80% of the state's small hog farms had closed from the early 1980's to the late 1990's, while the number of hogs had more than quadrupled to over ten million and passed the population of the state by 1995. That same year, after heavy rains, an eight-acre lagoon came down, allowing 25.8 million gallons of pig waste into the New River, killing 14,000 fish. Down river from the spill, 364,000 acres of wetlands had to be closed to shellfishing- permanently in some areas. Pfiesteria, named for the single-celled Dinoflagellate, is the culprit. Pfiesteria piscicida- Latin for "fish killer" is evident along the entire East Coast, but the overwhelming majority of outbreaks-and fish kills-have been consistently in the brackish waters of North Carolina. There, rivers like the Neuse, Pamlico and Chowan run from the states hog-heaviest zones to the oceanic estuaries nestled inside North Carolina's Outer Banks. In the summer of 1991, the year pfiesteria was identified by aquatic botanist Jeanne Burkholder, more than one billion fish in North Carolina were killed by it. In the years since, the annual pfiesteria-kill average runs at "several million," according to Burkholder and Rick Dove, an attorney and full-time river keeper for the Neuse River Basin. Dove should know. After retiring as a military judge for the U.S. Marines in 1987, he became a fisherman in the Neuse River estuary system. By 1990, however, he was forced to close his seafood operations because, as he puts it, "the fish population began to fall, and many of the fish I did catch were sick."

Nicknamed the "cell from hell", pfiesteria speedily multiplies, devastates fish populations, then dissipates, often with 24 hours. The microbe is thought to attack the fish's central nervous system, eat their skin and tissue, and cause bleeding ulcerated sores, although not all of these wounds have been linked to the microorganism. Some medical publications have stated that pfiesteria is also damaging to human cognitive processes. Burkholder would likely agree. She was forced to abandon experiments of the microbes for several weeks after experiencing memory loss, weakness, an inability to learn, headaches, and lesions similar to those found on the fish. How bad was it? Burkholder said on one occasion, working without proper protection, "I couldn't learn, speak, or remember for eight days. My assistant had long-term memory loss for three months. He couldn't remember where he lived-or even his phone number."

Where is the roadblock to fixing the problem? Our policies are often dictated by those willing to pay the most for them. In the 1996 election, hog farmers contributed more than $420,000 to state candidates. By 1998, farmers had formed an organization that spent $480,000 on lobbying and other political expenditures, and $2.6 million on pork friendly ads. In return, North Carolina Governor Jim Hunt, naturally a Democrat, proposed a bill, estimated at a minimum of $400 million, that would require taxpayers to foot 90% of the cost over the ten-year period. Do you think the Governor was obligated to anyone? The State Board of Elections ruled in 1998 that "Farmers for Fairness," a lobbying group for big hog operations, had illegally operated as a political action committee. Acting like Big Tobacco, the "hogsters" passed on a compromise anti-hog 1997 bill.

As usual, the government has done a poor job in oversight. The EPA has failed to track hundreds of thousands of pollution contaminating rivers, lakes and streams. An EPA inspector general saw it this way: "The system for tracking pollution permits and compliance is "incomplete, inaccurate, and obsolete." There has been no major overhaul since 1982. The EPA doesn't monitor thousands of major pollution sources, such as large hog farms and sewers that overflow during storms. It also does not require states to track the sources. Regulators know that dirty runoff from farms, storms and roads is a major source of water pollution, but they continue to focus only on the large facilities."

A portion of the defense made by hog farmers is that municipal water treatment plants are contributing to the dangerous spills. While true, the approach is still similar to the Clinton style of blaming someone else or trying to state that "everyone does it." Regardless, the spills had reached ridiculous numbers in North Carolina. In 1998, there were 774 spills, totaling 226 million gallons of raw sewage.

The problem is too close to my (former) home, but let me finish with a story of another's home. Karen Priest lives in a town outside Elizabethtown, NC, where she began to notice the stench that had kept her family hostage since the summer of 1994. Two industrial hog farms, one housing 7,300 hogs, the other 6,000-sprang up in 1994 within a mile of Priest's home. When the waste effluent of 13,000 hogs roll into the lagoons on the farm's in Priest's neighborhood, it's the equivalent of having more than

40,000 people living within a mile of their home-all using open sewers.

It's Tuesday afternoon in autumn and the redheaded Priest, comfortable in a baggy suit and jeans, is seated in the living room of her rambling family home. All the windows are shut against the smell of the hogs-which, at the moment, has thankfully subsided. In fact, the windows of the house have not been opened, Priest says, for four years. In the room with her are 15 neighbors, there to discuss their common problem. William McNeil, a quiet and dignified college professor, lives in an old farmhouse that is downwind from a hog operation. "My well's drinking water now exceeds EPA acceptable levels," he says, "it got that way after the hogs arrived. And the air? Often the smell permeates my house, even with the windows closed."

This "shit" can't go on. The hog industry produces <u>19 million tons</u> of hog waste per year. Studies show that 2/3 of the lagoons leak. What the hell is it going to take for us to stop this raping of our countryside, waterways, and maybe even water supplies, so a few people can get "filthy rich?" Way too much damage has already been done. As I have said earlier, "Pay attention and get involved." Otherwise, you'll leave your families what you deserve-a big pile of hog shit.

PROGRESS????????

"In 1995, N.C. Gov. Jim Hunt said that lagoons would be gone in 10 years. In 1997, the General Assembly said lagoons should be gone in five years. In 2000, Gov. Mike Easley said the lagoons would be gone in three years. Lagoons will never be eliminated until a date certain for complete phase-out is legislatively set. It's time for the clock to start ticking. Alternative technologies are available and becoming more affordable. It's time to get started."

RICK DOVE-New Bern, NC April 2007

CHAPTER EIGHT

INSURANCE SUCKS

Y CAREER EXPOSED me to all types of people in nearly every profession. While trying to avoid a rigid stereotype of people and their careers, I am able to define an accurate description of several "select" professions. I'll bet you can guess my first choice of profession. Nearly without exception, I have found that those people who made their living in the life insurance business are self-centered, only donate with the interest of a return, and when you reach the depth of their characters, you find their ass. Unfortunately, I have one perfect case description. Early in my career at the Rams Club, a group of people headed by an insurance agent, whose first initial is appropriately "F", proposed a gift that was substantial, but spread over nearly 20 years. Due to the amount of time necessary to receive the money and the awarding of certain up front priorities,

I did not think that the Rams Club should accept the proposal. My boss at the time was a good-natured man who operated more on the premise of securing the gift and worrying about the potential problems at a later date. In earlier years, this philosophy was more appropriate, but we were now asking people to donate specific amounts for specific priorities. While the fund-raising campaign at that time was not progressing quite as well as we had hoped, it was not necessary to make a deal like this one. The proposal was drawn up for the administrators to sign; and I refused. "F" was apparently less than pleased and called my boss to suggest that he should fire me. You can bet I did not forget this incident. "F" is still around, mellowing a bit, but the deep down character is still there. During my last year of working, there was a problem with his tickets being delivered (he probably pissed off the mailman) and he believed our staff was not responding to his self-centered needs. After we resolved the matter, he requested some thing of a personal meeting between the two of us. While not thrilled with the prospect of spending any time with him, I agreed to the meeting. My plan was to "close the door and air it out" with the understanding that it is two people talking, not the relationship between a donor and a Rams Club staff member. "F" said he would call for an appointment, but he never did before I retired. My buddy "F", unfortunately, is not an isolated example. Other donors with insurance ties are the people who will want to order their tickets late, complain the most and who push for more than they deserve from their priority. I guess it takes a certain type of person to be successful in the business of life insurance, one who often sells a product people do not need, or certainly less of it than necessary, and who are often just plain scam artists. Another case is one of two brothers that are both donors. Every call was from the guy is a problem; he is a local and I personally have never heard anyone say anything good about him. At the local country club, he approached a threesome getting ready to tee off and asked if he could join them. The reply was "no thanks, we already have our three." Since golf is mostly played in foursomes, it is obvious that the brother was deliberately rebuffed because of his personality. I advanced the idea of just giving people like "F" and the brother all of their donated money back to them. The staff would have to be better off and other members of the Rams Club would not have to be around those people. It works for me.

In another exhibition of the greed of the business, insurance underwriters showed extreme concern over Republican efforts to eliminate the inheritance death tax. In a report to members, the Association for Advanced Life Underwriting warned of a "devastating political development" if the Republican nominee for President was elected (Bush). Appropriately, Congressional Republicans fired back, "We find it "devastating" that you would work against the interests of estate-planning clients in order to protect your own member's livelihoods." Note-Democrats are still trying to keep the "death" tax.

I know you would be disappointed if the life insurance salesman were the only group highlighted in this chapter. I would be too. Risk management and related businesses are fields where the

"PIA's" (Pains in the Ass) are prevalent. These people are pushy and like to try and tell you how to run your business. They're looking for an angle, a better deal with the Rams Club being the loser. Real estate, with the men outperforming the women, is my last target. This is a business I would like to change, and I am not alone. Since I started this writing, there has been substantial growth in the number of realtors offering discount commissions. There have been legal challenges to the "standard" commission charged for the sale of real estate. Fortunately, the competition among the estimated 2.5 million real estate agents has helped drop the average commission from just over six percent to near five percent. In other countries, the average rate is some 25% less, and in the U.K. it is just two percent.

Help U Sell and Assist 2 Sell are two options that have shown up as an alternative to the old style real estate company and appropriately so. With higher prices and a median home price that had more than doubled over the last 25 years, the 6% commission figure does need adjustment. Are the agents doing that much more work to justify earning that much more per sale? I doubt it, although in the present real estate market of late 2007 my feelings may not be quite so strong. Regarding the Rams Club, the realtor contributors were frequently late with everything related to donations and tickets. This tardiness may not appear important, but when the total process of assigning tickets must be completed, a number of late orders can significantly impede progress in the task. To a very large degree, the same people were late every year.

While I won't target salespeople as a whole, I do want to tell you about one in particular. I went to high school with him, and he was disliked by nearly everyone. Basically, he was an "ass". While in high school, he was asked by his mother to help with getting golf clubs for his father. A friend of his had a father in the golf business, so the "ass" asked his friend to get some clubs. The father got his clubs, but only after the "ass" had marked up the price to his mother. "Ass" became a contributor to the Rams Club, but was a constant pest before each game trying to get last-minute better seats. Then, he made a commitment for a larger gift, only to withdraw it within a couple of years, indicating he was misled about some of the benefits and didn't want to get caught up in a money game. Misled, my ass, he was trying to squeeze the Rams Club as he has everything and everybody in his life. In my letter to him outlining the withdrawal of certain benefits, I tactfully, but with no lack of clarity, requested that he not come by the office in the future for any last-minute exchange of tickets.

People who solely focus on money are, in my observation, rarely satisfied as nearly every facet of their life revolves around the dollar. People like this do not listen well, generally have little empathy for others and make most people uncomfortable with their skewed focus. Two people that I know well have these characteristics, and I have never seen them either relaxed or happy. Hey guys, those extra few dollars aren't going to do you much good if you begin a dirt nap on short notice as a result of self-induced stress reducing your life span.

GOVERNOR CHARLIE CRIST

"I'm going to continue to do everything I can to push this industry into a direction of treating consumers fairly in the state of Florida. And right now-there are exceptions-but right now, they're not treating our citizens fairly, they're too greedy."

INSURANCE CORRUPTION???????

While Elliott Spitzer was the N.Y. Attorney General, he launched an investigation of the insurance industry in the state. The insurance industry is largely exempt from federal anti-trust enforcement under the McCarran-Ferguson Act of 1945. It left regulation to the states, and Spitzer determined there were abuses occurring in New York. "It is clear the federal government's hand-off policy with regard to insurance, combined with uneven state regulation has not entirely worked. Many state regulators have not been sufficiently aggressive in terms of supervising this industry." A Newsday editorial read "Until now, regulators looked the other way while insurers fleeced corporate policy holders."

In November of 2004, five executives at three insurance companies pled guilty to criminal fraud. Spitzer accused insurance broker Marsh and McLennan of bid rigging, price fixing and taking payoffs from insurers, like a kickback. Two AIG (American International Group) executives pled guilty. While announcing the action, Spitzer said "There is simply no responsible argument for a system that rigs bids, stifles competition and cheats customers." Spitzer urged a Senate Committee to dig deeper into the insurance issue, claiming lawmakers would find a "Pandora's box" of unethical conduct in coverage from automobile insurance to health-care benefits.

Good work, Elliott, and it helped you win the governor's race. Not such a good plan on trying to let the illegal immigrants get driver's licenses. But, none of that compares to being Client Number Nine in the prostitution scandal, which makes you one of the largest hypocrites in recent history.

CHAPTER NINE

DAN, I'D RATHER NOT SEE YOU ANYMORE (THE MEDIA SUCKS)

IN ORDER TO get good reviews for the book, I thought this would be an appropriate name for a chapter. Actually, my disgust for the media started when Dan Rather took over for Walter Cronkite on the "CBS Evening News." It seemed to me that over night that the news took on a less objective and more liberal tint. Unfortunately, I also lost respect for Cronkite when he was with Bill Clinton during the impeachment saga. Fortunately, due mostly to cable television (especially Fox) and the internet, there have been other options created to receive the news. In addition, a number of talk shows are available to cover important news in greater detail.

Since I started with Dan Rather, and I am interested in what he saw on the original Zapruder film of the Kennedy assassination, let me focus on his biased role in the 1992 election. Clinton was on the ropes as information regarding his affair with Gennifer Flowers began to make news. Just as Clinton did with Monica Lewinsky, he had suggested to Flowers that she deny, deny, deny. Over 300 newspapers called for Clinton to resign after his testimony in the Lewinsky case. I wish they had handled impeachment in the same manner.

I am going to use a few details from a letter from Graham Marlette to the "Durham Morning Herald," which used to be my local newspaper. Marlette states, "The national news networks are in a unique position of power. They choose which stories to report, when to report them, and how to spin the details to suit their particular bias, if they have one. CBS has raised it to an art form. "Contextualizing the news" is what Dan Rather calls it, and it amounts to an assumption that the public is too stupid to know what's going on." As I wrote the chapter about our nation's schools, I realized Dan may have been more right than wrong.

Dan had done some good investigation work in the past, "but it just doesn't compensate for what viewers perceive as a monumental ego, a journalist who sees himself as both king-maker and dragon-slayer, determined to move America to the left, whether it wants to go there or not. He lacks credibility because we see in retrospect that, in effect, he lied about the economy during the presidential election campaign of 1992.

He knew that the seeds of our present prosperity were sown by Republicans, but Rather does not like Republicans and did not like their candidate, George Bush. So he decided to do his part and use the evening news program to ensure Bush's defeat. Night after night, curiously close to election time, he trotted out attractive young couples who had recently been down sized, lost their up-scale California homes, and were being victimized by the economy. It was not a news story, it was a feature, but Rather was determined to bring down George Bush (actually both father & son) and what better backdrop for this deception than voter-rich California?

For Bush to lose, Clinton has to win and Rather spotted a potential problem: A women named Gennifer Flowers is now claiming that candidate Clinton is a long-term adulterer. Facing the problem head-on, CBS conducts an interview with the candidate and his wife. Viewers are treated to an outraged Hillary, affecting her now-famous fake Southern accent. She declared that she was no stand-by-your-man Tammy Wynette, and if her hubby was turning tricks with a blonde floozy, she would be the first to know about it. It appears that Hillary was not the first to know about Monica, but how could she really be surprised? Her husband himself admitted that he had participated in hundreds of affairs. On TV, with Dan watching over him, Clinton said he didn't do it. (LIAR) Period. End of story.

That was more than enough for Rather. It would be a stretch to give Rather all the credit for the Clinton victory. George Bush made his own contribution, but failing to report on a candidate's serious character flaws and lying about the economy is more than bad journalism. It's an abuse of power." (just like Clinton) Footnote-according to one study, some 90% of the media voted for Clinton.

Thanks, Graham. After this book is published, you get a free copy from the author, if you want to request one.

As Dan got his way in the 1992 election, he was absolutely giddy when talking with the Clintons early in their first term. "If we could be one-hundredth as great as you and Hillary Rodham Clinton have been in the White House, we'd take it right now and walk away as winners." This was Dan talking, in May of 1993, about his new on-air partnership with Connie Chung. Need any more evidence? What was he doing at a Democrat fund-raiser in March of 2000? If CBS had any sense of propriety, Dan would have been appropriately disciplined. All of these incidents pale in comparison, of course, to the false document report on George Bush and his National Guard service, brought out just weeks before the 2004 election. Michael Goodwin of the N.Y. Daily News wrote "Make no mistake. Something very bad and damaging happened here, and not just to CBS. Coming during a nasty election, the shame of **Rathergate** has eroded Americans fragile trust in all news organizations." Dan's bias finally caught up to him, and he lost his anchor job. Now, he is suing CBS for $180 million. Dan, time to go to pasture. You're done.

Because of people like Rather, many Americans are searching outside the networks for their news. As early as 1998, cable viewership exceeded ABC, CBS, NBC, and Fox combined. The volume of Internet traffic was doubling every 100 days, and seven million new households were going "on line" annually. The network's primetime audience was also down, by nine percent, in 1998. Newspaper circulation had fallen from 63.1 million in 1984 to 56.7 million in 1997. In Boston, the top three newscasts dropped by 50,000 households in just one year. The Boston Globe and Boston Herald weekday circulation declined 10% and 25% in the 90's. The media is controlled by large corporations presenting the news based on their prejudices. Stories often reflect the social views of reporters and editors rather than any non-partisan or objective standard.

These prejudices were overly evident in the non-stop coverage of the plane search for John Kennedy Jr. For the media, the Kennedys are royalty. Several network anchors became personal in their grief. "The Kennedys are our family too," choked one overwrought correspondent. Media big shots are part of a tiny elite that circulates with other members of the elite and has only a limited understanding of ordinary people. It was a horrible tragedy, but the media simply lost their heads.

Quotas. I have always believed that using quotas on hiring, etc. was contrary to equal opportunity. It is difficult to believe that quotas became operative in the media. John Leo, another of my favorites, reveals in "U.S. News" in late June of 1998 that Mark Willes, publisher of the "Los Angeles Times" told the "Wall Street Journal" that he intended to set specific goals for the numbers of women and men quoted in his newspaper. As Leo noted, "this is an ominous idea, sure to compromise the integrity of any paper that tries it." While Leo believes that "dusty Rolodex syndrome" may be a factor, where reporters tend to keep quoting the same sources, he quickly focuses on the fact that Willes didn't just say, "Let's expand our Rolodexes and make an effort to quote relevant people from all sorts of backgrounds." In effect, he said he was installing a by-the-numbers system of affirmative action quoting. He told the Journal that if a reporter is "writing about steel or Barbie dolls or international trade or human rights in China, and you can't find a quality woman or minority to quote, then I will."

Reporters on deadline might worry about not having an Asian American or a gay person quoted in their copy. And Willes plan is backed up by economic pressure. Raises and promotions would be withheld from editors if reporters fail to meet designated numbers.

Like all affirmative-action plans, Willes's plan downgrades merit in favor of group representation. Human-interest stories are relatively easy to include a broad range of people, but with technical or breaking news, reporters should be focused on securing the best experts or most relevant sources. Unfortunately, they will be worrying about filling their race-and-gender bingo cards with somebody, anybody, from every designated group. With concern for spreading the pieces of a story among the groups, the meaning of a report can easily be blurred by parceling out the viewpoints.

Reporters for the "Times" worried that they have to identify everyone's ethnic identity. Phone interviews, presumably, had to include questions about ethnicity or skin color. How much diversity is needed? Inevitably, affirmative-action plans in the newsroom are based on a condensed version of diversity-women, blacks, Indians, gays, Hispanics and Asian-Americans, but not recent Russian or Irish immigrants, Jews, Muslims, or conservative Christians. Catherine Seipp, a Los Angeles journalist, writes that in a story about housing prices, "a quote from a happy homeowner who's also a Persian Jew would be unlikely to get a bonus for anyone."

Leo believes that the quotas leave the "implication that each ethnic and sexual group has a distinct group perspective that all members share or ought to share," and for most stories this does not make sense. What it does do is "create the impression that almost all news should be viewed through prisms of race and gender."

It is refreshing that the Willes plan met some heavy resistance at the "Times". A meeting between Willes and the staff was described as "contentious", "confrontational", "lively", and "vigorous". Some felt that Willes was only a bottom-line businessman (he came from a cereal company) trying to impose a crude plan on the newsroom. Apparently, the idea for the affirmative action quoting had been simmering for years. In fact, a "Times" diversity committee was mandated, some seven years previously, to "examine the demographic nature of sources."

Reporters from some papers are being required to complete forms of whether the stories have been "mainstreamed" (euphemism for quoting by quota). Performance evaluations judge editors and reporters by "diversity friendliness" or how they fill out "diversity checklists."

One of the checklists that made rounds at various newspapers asked, "Am I furthering stereotypes as I seek diversity?" and "Am I battling stereotypes?" This appears to imply that reporters are properly engaged in social engineering, not just gathering news.

Because of the rising "diversity" pressures, reporters will tend to go along to protect their careers, censoring certain ideas, avoiding certain stories and meandering away from straight reporting whenever necessary to satisfy the checklist enthusiasts.

This is not a narrow dispute at a single newspaper. It's a broad story about what the diversity movement is doing to the news. William McGowan, in his book, "Coloring the News" laments that the political homogeneity that the movement has wrought, citing numerous examples with detailed documentation.

So while you question whether the stories you are reading are more diversity than fact, you also need to know about four major newspaper incidents, including reporters fabricating people in their stories and a newspaper paying $10 million to settle any legal claims. "The Cincinnati Enquirer" agreed to pay Chiquita Brands more than $10 million and issued a front-page apology after a report questioning the company's business practices was partially based on 2,000 internal voice-mail messages that were stolen from Chiquita.

Other incidents: the "New Republic" fired reporter Steve Glass after an internal investigation determined fabricated parts of or all of 27 of the 41 articles he had written. Glass's fictionalized accounts were so dazzling that "George", "Harpers", and "Rolling Stone" also printed his work.

As columnist Robert Scheer states, "The problem is to be found throughout in the widespread acceptance of unnamed sources as the basis for stories. Without any track record, Glass was able to rise from the ranks of fact checker to "New Republic" senior editor and star writer because his fibs fed the Washington gossip mill."

Even prize-winning journalism has been based on fictionalized sourcing. "The Boston Globe" reporter Patricia Smith, a Pulitzer Prize finalist and winner of a 1997 American Society of Newspaper Editors distinguished award, invented a dying cancer patient whose compelling story she told. After an internal review revealed that she had made up quotes and people in four columns, the paper asked her to resign.

An area where the media has played a dangerous role is the reporting of terrorism. Dan Thomasson of Scripps Howard News Service writes in September 2007 that "Every time Osama Bin Laden's propaganda machine cranks up, he is immediately awarded star status. Talk about aiding and abetting the goals of one's enemy. The latest Bin Laden video is little more than a call to recruit fanatics to his cause, which is, of course, to rid the world of as many of us and our allies as possible. The haste of mainline distributors of our news to hit the airways or headlines with Bin Laden's every word exceeds the boundaries of good journalism." Until he is gone, "it can only be wished that those who understand that he is a cave-dwelling, murderous misanthrope will use better judgment in allowing him a periodic platform to address the people of a nation he hates. But don't bet on it."

Now to Hollywood, and help from Sara Eckel. She says "those in Hollywood say it is fashionable that Hollywood never made anyone pick up a gun, that the people who do kill would have done so anyway and copycat crimes merely reflect the lack of creativity on part of the criminals." I see why these people love Bill Clinton. Always blame someone else.

"This is nonsense. The entertainment media convey a sense of what is within the realm of the possible. A major study released in April of 2001 by Dr. Susan Villani, a psychiatrist at Johns Hopkins University, showed that viewers of violent TV learned aggressive behavior and attitudes, became desensitized to violence, and became fearful of being victimized. A preference for heavy metal music in the 1990's was linked to stealing, driving fast, using drugs and becoming sexually promiscuous as an adolescent. If everyone on prime-time television is sleeping around, there is no question that influences the viewer's sense of what is proper and acceptable. Several years ago, "The Money Train" portrayed a criminal fire-bombing the ticket booth of a New York subway. Within a few weeks of the movie's release, three copycat crimes had occurred. Harry Kaufman, who worked inside one of these booths, was condemned to days of torture from third-degree burns and ultimately death.

The veneer of civilization is very thin. Almost all of us have the capacity under the right circumstances to behave savagely, as evidenced by the teenage suicide bombers in the Middle East. Some of us need only a little encouragement.

Clearly, the causes of violence are complex. But there have always been tormented teenagers. Only recently have they thought it reasonable to blow their classmates away with shotguns. If I were a Hollywood producer who put before the eyes of impressionable kids images that glorify violence and revel in pornography (the sexual and violent kind), I would find it awfully hard to sleep at night."

Sara, a very thoughtful article. You, like many others with Creators Syndicate, have inspired me to write this book and proudly use your words of wisdom.

This brings me to more media abuse from "The New York Times," a constant source of biased reporting, as well as the leaking of sensitive government information. President Bush asked the paper not to publish the story about the NSA (National Security Agency) eavesdropping on certain U.S. citizen's phone calls, a process that, among others, prevented a blowup of the Brooklyn Bridge in 2003.

The paper helped inflame and sustain protests over the police shooting of Amadou Diallo in New York City in 1999, averaging 3.5 Diallo stories per day for two months! On the day the indictments were leaked, there were nine stories. As Heather McDonald of the "City Journal" wrote, "The Diallo crisis was a manufactured one-an unparalleled example of the power of the press, and above all, the N.Y. Times, to create the reality it reports." In Cincinnati, the media attempted to downplay the rioting by blacks over the shooting of a black man. Calling the riots "sporadic protests and vandalism," the media, particularly "The N.Y. Times," ignored the fact that there were more than 100 hours of gunshots and businesses set on fire. A mob of black youths dragged a white woman from her car and beat her until neighborhood residents rescued her. Another albino black woman was hit by bricks, including one to the head. Her attack stopped when someone yelled, "she's black." Sounds like a riot to me.

The media coverage revolved around one endlessly recycled fact that Cincinnati police had killed 15 black people in six years.

Negating the "Time" magazine statement that "Cincinnati had become a model of racial injustice" is a series that the "The Cincinnati Enquirer" did on the police in 1999. The conclusions were that there were no unusual racial patterns. Seventy-eight percent of the people who were shot were black, and the same percentage of violent felonies were committed by blacks. The department was roughly one-quarter black, and the same percentage of police shootings were by black officers.

Trying to influence the 2000 presidential election, the media tried to paint George W. Bush as dumb. The same tactic was tried on Ronald Reagan, reflecting journalist prejudices about Republicans in general. You probably will not get too many personal admissions, but conventional wisdom among elites today is that Reagan was a successful president. Early in the war in Afghanistan, the media did their best to describe the conflict in "Vietnam"-like terms, excessively using the word quagmire. An October 31, 2001 headline in "The New York Times" read "A Military Quagmire remembered: Afghanistan as Vietnam." Different times, different war strategies, and great initial success by the U.S. and its allies in Afghanistan.

Also on the political front, we were served up "The West Wing" on television. Despite some excellent acting, the show was an obvious attempt to portray a Clinton White House if Clinton had been monogamous. The steady ratings deadline indicated that others besides me grew weary of the show that began somewhat realistically, but morphed into a political statement. With left-wing activist Martin Sheen as the president, this was not a surprise. Republicans were portrayed as bad, just like in the 1995 movie, "An American President," where a hateful Republican presidential candidate charges the Democrat with sexual charges.

ARE WE CATCHING ON?

I have already mentioned William McGowan's book, "Coloring the News," but also wanted to note the great courage of Bernard Goldberg, who worked at CBS. I highly recommend his book: "Bias: A CBS Insider Exposes How the Media Distorts the News", published in 2003. As a result of the book, to no one's surprise, Dan Rather turned on his former friend, Goldberg, effectively freezing him out of reporting on the evening news. Bernie, thanks, and I think it was better that you got away from Dan anyway. Let me also give a thumbs-up to Bernie's other books "Arrogance-Rescuing America from the Media Elite", " 110 People Who are Screwing Up America", and "Crazies to the Left of Me, Wimps to the Right", and for his ongoing excellent television work.

A big surprise on the media watch was the Tammy Bruce book, "The New Thought Police: Inside the Left's Assault on Free Speech and Free Minds." Bruce is a former president of the Los Angeles chapter of NOW (National Organization for Women), is pro-abortion and an activist lesbian. However, she campaigned against the gay and lesbian drive to get conservative "Dr. Laura" off television. According to Bruce, rampant "political correctness" is limiting the diversity of views on college campuses, Hollywood, and on television.

I like the trends here, on the Internet, Fox and other locales, and hope more people will pay attention to the search for truth. Mark Twain gave us the warning, "A lie will travel half-way around the world while the truth is putting on its shoes." Technology and choice are changing the life span of the lies.

L.A. TIMES UPDATE

Weekday circulation has dropped by 300,000 in the last seven years. I guess the Willes plan hurt the paper.

CHAPTER TEN

RELIGION AND TRADITION

THIS CHAPTER MAY anger as many as any other, but remember I said that this book would not be pleasing to everyone.

The portion on religion will be relatively short. I was basically forced to attend church until graduating from high school. While I believed in the discipline of my parents, I also felt that religion was a very personal matter that should be left to personal preference after, perhaps, elementary school age. I grew to resent being forced to make every Sunday a ritual of getting out of bed to go to church. This resentment could have been aggravated by a few Sunday hangovers in high school.

Religion, like tradition, can grow stale. While hearing the minister read from the Bible, I began to lose interest after hearing many of the verses in repetition. I understood their intent and did not need to hear someone read it to me. Sure, there was the infrequent enjoyable sermon, such as the one on the song, "Let It Be", but that was not enough to maintain my interest. I don't feel that you need to go to church to make yourself a better person, but should strive to achieve the basic goals of the Bible in everyday life, particularly the Golden Rule of treating people the way you would like to be treated. Unfortunately, this rule is too often abused and ignored, often by many of the people that attend church regularly. I did see a number of hypocrites who were regular in their church attendance, and, in this case, I am striving not to be judgmental, but instead objectively observant. The key psychological difference between religious and non-religious people is that the former crave interdependence, while the latter have a strong desire to be self-reliant and independent. That is according to an Ohio State University study. I have seen those consumed by the church. Rather than using the church as a support for their value system, it is used as an emotional crutch. This is dangerous and unhealthy. What happens is personalities are lost or blurred, and the sense of objectivity is significantly obscured. The worst part is that some individuals and some churches prey on the vulnerability of many of these people, and there is a local (near Chapel Hill) church guilty of this practice. This reminds me of the days of Jim Bakker and the PTL Club. Jim and Tammy, his wife with five pounds of makeup, had a local TV show on Sunday nights. It was remarkable, then, to see Jim and Tammy plead for contributions for what seemed to be personal gain, not to aid those who needed help from the church. More remarkably, people sent their money as the Bakkers amassed a huge fortune. My friends and I saw the Bakkers in quite a different light, often calling the show to verbally abuse Jim and his scamming of the viewers. Thankfully, Jim ended up in prison, but what about the millions he raked in from trusting contributors? Then, as now, I am fearful of the number of people who are both uninformed and unable to manage their lives individually.

As he has been such a positive influence on my life in numerous ways, it did not surprise me that Paul McCartney had an appropriate definition of religion. In an interview in the late 1980's, he was asked, "Do you have any strong religious views?" No, I am generally against religions, because it is factions. Religious groups eventually get to that. I have a very simplistic view of it. I got this idea that God was good with an o taken out, and the devil was evil with a d added. I figure if I do something really evil, something will get me. I believe in the spirit of good and the spirit of evil."

Please let me make it clear that religion can be a most helpful base of support for numerous people. The church is often the beginning point of many charitable services. The problem exists in the extremes, those who seemed to be consumed, and really lost within the church, and those who use it as an excuse to abuse the message of the Bible. Then, the abusers hide behind their phony beliefs. Bill Clinton would be one example.

Tradition, in my view, is overrated. I would acknowledge that an event like the Masters golf tournament has an appreciative tradition, particularly when compared to other sporting events. At the time of this writing, the cost of tickets for the four-day tournament was $100. There were only four television sponsors, which limit commercials to only a total of four minutes per hour. The cost of food at the event is about 20% of the cost at other major tournaments. Parking costs nothing, and there are no corporate tents. A contrast is the Atlantic Coast Conference (ACC) Men's Basketball Tournament, which used to be an appealing "fan" event. Today, excessive media coverage and a substantial corporate presence have significantly diminished the event. The Final Four is further down the same road, even to the point of taking many of the best tickets away from the participating schools, selling them in a "hospitality package". More simply put, they are scalping tickets that should be going to the participating schools, and somehow trying to hide behind a counterfeit ticket excuse. Sad, and it needs to be stopped. In 1998, Carolina received 4,500 tickets to the Final Four in San Antonio. This year, they only got 3,250 tickets, and 1,000 of the 1,250 ticket reduction came from lower level seats. I hope an athletic director with "leadership skills" will lead a campaign to properly return the tickets to the schools.

Unfortunately, in most other cases, I believe tradition is more just the old way of doing things. Weddings would probably be first on my list. I feel certain that couples get back more from creating their own wedding, reception, etc., rather than relying on the old standard of doing things. Don't be afraid to come up with new ideas, for, after all, it is your wedding, not just a routine ceremony. It's not a great example, but my first wedding was held outside in an amphitheater beside a lake. My vows were original, although not recited well, and a song by Paul McCartney, although not played well, was included in the wedding. The wedding reception can certainly be another source of originality. I attended the wedding of one of the UNC ticket office employees several years ago. The reception was held at a private country club in Pinehurst. There was a disc-jockey, or something similar, lots of dancing by people of all ages, and then the newlyweds, both excellent golfers, drove off in a golf cart. Supposedly, even some of the guests at the reception drove in circles around the parking lot in the golf cart, but I don't personally recall that occurring.

Another function of tradition is those who profit from it. The businesses involved with weddings and debutante functions, such as tuxedo rentals, caterers, photographers, etc. seem to have localized monopolies. Rebecca Mead, in her book "One Perfect Day-The Selling of the American Wedding says that the annual $161 billion wedding industry (includes total spent for honeymoon, presents, purchases and insurance) has created "Bridezilla," the out of control bride. Mead believes that the photographers, planners and others prey on the bride's fears of an imperfect wedding. I have seen numerous couples and ex-wives agonize over all facets of the wedding, and the celebration of getting married is lost in the worry about food, suits, dresses, photo shots and the average cost of $26,000. My suggestion is to go small on the actual wedding, have a party at some time, if you desire, and save the difference in expenses for a longer and likely more memorable honeymoon. I probably just lost a few sales from those in the wedding business, but it would be worth it for the new couples to have more fun.

My second example of tradition for deletion is from my fraternity at Carolina. As a pledge during my freshman year, the entire "pledge class" had to spend several days sleeping in our chapter room, which was in the basement of an old house. We couldn't take a shower, could only eat certain food, and had various worthless rituals each night. All of this preceded the "initiation" of officially becoming a member. Rather than being excited about the moment of becoming a "brother", I definitely resented the complete process. It did not make me appreciate the opportunity of becoming a member. The freshman year at an academically challenging school like Carolina is difficult enough without the addition of a degrading ritual of tradition.

Conclusion; take some to create new celebrations. How much can it really hurt you to try something different?

LETTERS FROM AMERICA

Prosecute religious groups

"I don't understand why churches and other religious groups think they can put their doctrine ahead of the laws of our country by harboring illegal immigrants. We live in a nation governed by laws. Any religious group violating our laws should have its non-profit status revoked, and the individuals responsible for the violations prosecuted to the fullest extent of the law."

RON SUTTON-Orlando, FL

CHAPTER ELEVEN

OUR SCHOOLS ARE TERRIBLE-WHO'S TO BLAME?

A LARGE, LARGE PERCENTAGE of the many problems covered in this book can be reduced or eliminated with appropriate and ongoing education. First, it is incumbent upon parents to insist that their children are educated properly. Properly means to guide the youth of our country in the pursuit of an education that is meaningful and productive. At present, there is enormous blame to be shared by many people and organizations. Our entire educational system is in need of revision, from the bureaucracy in Washington to the teacher unions to the state bureaucracies to…... even some teachers. The bloated bureaucracies are evident in numbers released by the Hoover Institution in 2005. Only eleven states had at least 65% of their operational budgets reach the classroom, 15 had less than 60%, and Washington, DC was less than 50%. Guess the DC'ers were too close to that bigger bloated bureaucracy.

Without the proper education, everyone is being deprived of living a complete life. The education, however, is not simply the attendance of school for children. It should be the daily goal of everyone to continuously educate themselves. This means being aware of your local community as well as national and world affairs. I refer to the Rush Limbaugh description of the "informed vs. the uninformed," which is an accurate definition of the problem. While not dismissing the vital importance of raising and educating children, it is also paramount for adults to stay informed to help them make proper decisions for the welfare of their children, their own lives and their country.

First of all, I feel the need to stress how awful the educational problem is for our country. In 1983, members of the National Commission on Excellence on Education wrote "if an unfriendly foreign power had attempted to impose on America the mediocre educational performance that exists today, we might have viewed it as an act of war." Little has changed since the commission's report, "A Nation at Risk," was released. In John Leo's article in the March 9, 1998 "U.S. News & World Report," titled "Hey, we're No. 19," the pitiful results of the Third International Mathematics & Science Study, ranked American high school seniors 19th of 21 countries in math and science scores. Unbelievably, the performance was actually worse than it looked, because Asian nations, which do particularly well in these comparisons, were not involved in this study. Otherwise, as Leo notes, we might have been fighting for 39th or 40th place in a 41 nation field. The very latest report by the Organization for Economic Development had the U.S. 17th in science and 24th in math. The most popular rationalization of low scores is that they are solely a reflection of the democratization of our educational system, but the opinion has no merit. Even our best students did poorly by world standards. American advanced students in math came in 15th, and American advanced science students came in 16th.

What does the U.S. system have that other national systems don't? For one, it tolerates a high number of unqualified and barely qualified teachers-almost a third of math teachers and half of physical science teachers do not major or minor in these subjects at college. Largely because of the culture of the teacher's colleges, our public education is pervaded by social attitudes that work against achievement. College instructors complain that large numbers of freshmen now arrive on campus ready to explain their feelings and attitudes, but unable to construct a rational argument.

Schools are flooded with so-called progressive and social agendas that either go down in flames or crowd out actual learning-cooperative learning, the politics of identity, outcome-based education, history as group therapy. This emphasis often has strange effects, making some teachers suspicious of achievement and any knowledge that "contributes to inequality." Some teachers now refer to themselves as "facilitators" because they believe "teaching" is an expansion of dominance.

As would be expected, the Democrat Party tries the old "buy the votes" trick with education. Who's backing them? You won't be surprised; it's the unions. Texas and several states attempted to inject more accountability into all phases of public education. Their common-sense argument: If students and teachers are being held to higher educational standards, why not the colleges that train educators, too? Under Texas law, teacher colleges that can't raise the graduation pass rates enough within two years, and remedial help is available, will be forced to close down. These tough sanctions are based on research linking teacher quality to student achievement. Studies show dramatic learning gains among students with the most knowledgeable teachers. Yet in some states, as many as 50% of college education majors fail state licensing exams.

Too often, these unlicensed teachers end up in classrooms anyway, through emergency waivers for school districts with high poverty rates, or growing districts that are unable to find enough qualified teachers. What do the unions want to do about these problems?

Both the NEA (National Education Association) and the AFT (American Federation of Teachers) have resisted efforts to make teachers more accountable and give parents more choice in the schools their children attend. School choice is a concept shared by blacks and whites, as well as raising academic standards and achievement. Eighty percent of black parents say the higher priority for schools should be higher standards and 51% say integrated schools make little difference in their child's education; the percentage for whites are 88% and 72% on the same statement. These results are from a poll of 1,600 parents, half black and half white, by the research group Public Agenda and reported in "USA Today" by Tamara Henry on July 29, 1998.

The two unions have also fought especially hard against school voucher programs and tuition tax credits for parents who want to send their children to private and parochial schools. As Linda Chavez notes in her July 9, 1998 editorial, "The NEA's first priority is electing politicians who will do the NEA's bidding in Congress, in state legislatures and on school boards." In 1998, this meant stopping efforts to expand voucher plans, which enable poor parents to pick the schools their children attend, just as more affluent parents do".

"Union officials warn that vouchers will destroy public education by creaming the best students from public schools, leaving the most difficult students behind. But that's nonsense. Catholic schools already educate large numbers of poor, urban, minority students whose parents sacrifice so their children can succeed." Average tuition at Catholic elementary schools runs about $1,600 a year and high school tuition, $3,600. Per-pupil spending on public education more than doubled from 1983-1999 to nearly $6,600, according to the U.S. Department of Education. Federal spending on education nearly doubled during the Clinton years of 1992-2000. Prior to the 2000 presidential election, the Department of Education, for months, sat on an impact study of 16,000 kindergartners, which showed that preschool programs, like Head Start, should emphasize *academic* skills. The most likely reason for the suppression? The study supported Bush's views about revamping Head Start.

Chavez reveals a study of 13 inner-city New York City schools, where Catholic schools graduated 95% of their students, compared with only about 50% graduation rates for city public schools. Some 85% of Catholic school students took the SAT exams for college students, while only 33% of the public school seniors took the tests. Yet, the overwhelmingly majority of Catholic school students (75%-90%, depending on the school) were black or Hispanic, as were the public school students. Chavez concludes, "perhaps a little competition from the Catholic and other private schools might jolt the unions into concentrating more on improving the quality of public education and less on electing politicians who make excuses for the failure of public education."

That competition, notes Mona Charen, should come from the benefits of capitalism. Yet, the education system lacks capitalism's driving engine: competition. Dr. Checker Finn, President of the Thomas B. Fordham Foundation and a leading education philosopher, proposed at a meeting of education reformers a list of reforms that would learn from other nation's successes as well as draw upon our own national strengths.

1.) Institute national assessments that would be independent of politics.

2.) Pass a charter school law in every state.

3.) Eliminate geography as a determinant of school assignment. Or, in other words, let parents choose their children's schools.

4.) Strap the money to the back of the child, that is, fund students, not schools.

5.) Don't force programs, like bilingual education, that parent's don't want.

6.) Use proven pedagogic methods and real curricula (no more whole language and whole math)

7.) Eliminate teachers who don't know their subjects.

8.) Offer merit pay for great teachers.

9.) Lengthen the school day or year-or both. (In Japan, students attend 220 days as compared to our 180).

10.) Include parents much more in running the schools, participating in classrooms and more.

As Leah Vukmir, director of Wisconsin's Parent Raising Educational Standards to Schools, noted, parents around the nation complain about the same problems-low standards, too little direct instruction, fad teaching methods and no accountability. Every parent who wants the best for his or her children, and every American who wants the best for the country, should seriously consider Finn's list. The competition produced dividends in Milwaukee schools, where an evaluation of the public schools by the Hoover Institution noted a strong productivity response to competition from vouchers. The evaluation clearly stated, "If we want more, better-educated graduates and more value for tax dollars, the solution is obvious-unleash competition."

The problems, of course, are not just a function of poor schools. It starts at home. Walter Williams addressed this issue in an editorial for Creator's Syndicate. As noted in the information about public school spending, our country, led by the Democrats, has been trying to improve education for decades by dumping billions of dollars into schools, equipment, books and teachers with little to show for it. Philadelphia is another prime example, where 176 out of 264 of the public schools were on a failing list. The state had to take over operation of the Philadelphia schools.

"Another assumption," notes Williams, "is that educational achievement depends on a multiplicative relationship between the home and the school. That is, educational achievement depends upon what happens in the home times (and the times is very important) what happens in school. In that case, if the home environment is worth zero, no matter what resources we put into schools, there's going to be disappointing results. That's because zero times anything of any magnitude equals zero."

Considerable evidence suggests a multiplicative relationship. Children who tend to do well in school generally come from two-parent families. In the book, "A New Generation of Evidence: The Family is Critical to Student Achievement," by Anne Henderson and Nancy Berla, it is revealed that 85 studies show profoundly that parental involvement unequivocally renders higher grades and test scores, better attendance and more thoroughly completed homework. Let's review those single-parent percentages by race again, black 70%, Hispanic 43%, white 30%. In 1965, a young Daniel Patrick Moynihan in his report, "The Negro Family," saw danger in the fact that some <u>25%</u> of new black births were to unwed new mothers. Again, some of the thanks can go to the great LBJ and his "Great Society" for perpetuating the cycle of despair for blacks.

"Parents ensure that homework is done and educational material is in the home. Children are lectured about school behavior and punished when necessary. Parents make sure they attend school every day and on time. Parents respond to school notices and grades. And, they make sure their kids go to bed at a reasonable hour.

A good home environment is vital to getting a good education. The measures that parents take to create a good home environment cannot be done by government or educators. If what only parents can do is not done, education results will always be disappointing. If you accept this vital multiplicative relationship between the home environment and the school, what are the policy recommendations?"

Even in the worst schools, there are kids whose parents provide a decent home environment. These kids, however, may not reach their academic potential because of the presence of other kids from poor home environments. "School administrators cannot prevent these kids from bringing the education process to a virtual halt. Instead of teacher's teaching, they spend most of their class time on discipline, trying to motivate hostile and alien minds and vainly attempting to help chronic truants to catch up."

"The educational establishment and the civil rights establishment (read most Democrats) seem to have the attitude that no kids shall be educated well until it is possible for all kids to be educated well." Where has this attitude gotten us? Roderick Page, the Secretary of Education in the Bush administration, stated that "125 billion dollars of Title I money was spent over the last 25 years with virtually nothing to show for it." Eighty billion was spent just in the 1990's, most of it in the Clinton years. The National Assessment of Educational Progress (NAEP), often called the "nation's report card" gave a grade of "F" for the last three decades of expensive "education reform." The report uses four levels of achievement, which are advanced, proficient, basic and below basic. Basic is defined as "cannot understand, even in a general sense, the meaning of what they have read." The simpler definition is "THEY CAN'T READ." Here are the ugly numbers: 63% of blacks, 58% of the Hispanics, 47% of the urban kids and 60% of the poor children are below basic. Conclusion: we are "looking at another lost generation."

In another Williams' (who is black) article, he writes that Clinton's "feeling our pain" and his race group talking up race did nothing for the real problems that stymie black progress. Clinton's agenda was to shore up political support among the black elite so they will guide their flock at the voting booth."

Does this sound familiar? Throw money at a problem, don't focus on the solutions, for the main purpose of "buying" support from a particular group. Damn, that "Great Society" plan biting us in the ass again. A study conducted by the accounting firm Coopers and Lybrand for the South Carolina Department of Education shows no correlation between the money spent in a district and SAT scores. Want more? Here are five states with the five highest SAT scores and their states ranking in per pupil expenditures in the year 2000: 1. North Dakota (41st) 2. Iowa (25th) 3. Wisconsin (10th) 4. Minnesota (16th) 5. South Dakota (48th). Blacks need to recognize this failed attempt to help them and Williams makes a strong case to try to "persuade" his race.

"Fraudulent education is the standard state of affairs for most black youngsters (it's not much better for whites). Despite this, black politicians, civil rights leaders, white liberals, and Democrats give government schools unquestioned support. Defenders argue that teachers and administrators cannot be held responsible for the gross sociological problems they encounter trying to teach kids from broken homes and violent, drug-infested neighborhoods. That's right. However, teachers and administrators have total control over what grades and diplomas are issued."

What do the black public-schools teachers think about their schools? Black teachers nationally are 50% more likely than black parents in general to use private school.

"Colleges cover up high-school fraud by admitting black students who have little prospect of graduating. College President's success for state money and fund-raising depends on "racial diversity"-having those black bodies on campus. In the case of Temple University, 90% of academically ill-prepared students, euphemized as "developmental students", fail to survive."

"Clinton's proposal for more education dollars for smaller classes did not do anything but enrich the education establishment (ATF, NEA). There will be no improvement until the average black parent says enough is enough and demands some form of school choice as a means to a callous, deceptive (Clinton specialty) education monopoly."

Vince Ellison, past president of the African-American Unity Conference in Columbia, SC has called for African-Americans to "abandon the failed policy of integration at all costs. Those of us who believe the public school system is not educating our children properly, we must demand the right to place them in havens that will adequately do the job. This can only be done through charter schools and school vouchers."

Parents, now it's your turn. I am going to keep this brief, as I want to believe most of you are asking many of the same questions and raising the same concerns addressed in this chapter. First of all, I have raised no kids of my own, so I don't qualify as an "expert in the field."

When I use the word "parents," I mean to emphasize that the utmost energy must be directed to decreasing the number of children born to unwed parents. Black leaders, and I do not mean the "Reverends" Jackson, Sharpton, and Farrakan, need to be in the forefront. General Colin Powell and the previously mentioned former Oklahoma congressman J.C. Watts are two leaders that I would recommend as models for the black community to follow. Perhaps, Senator Barack Obama may prove to be another. It is not possible to solve a complex problem unless you begin to attack it at the core. The elimination of ADC (Aid for Dependent Children) should be helpful, as well as the cutoff of welfare after two years. The Hispanics, the fastest growing portion of our population, need the same kind of leadership example, but a significant contribution to the problem could be made by enforced, heavy border control and enforcing the immigration laws.

FACTS TO LEAVE WITH YOU

This chapter could have easily been a whole book, but I was worried about keeping your attention and I was interested in many other subjects. The first person that reviewed my book suggested leaving out this chapter, because, "Everyone knows the educational system sucks." I wish he was right, but not enough people know or the movement for change would be stronger. Education is one area where the unions have really hurt this country. They should have a much smaller role in the process.

President Bush made education reform a cornerstone of his campaign, and made a good effort through the passage of an education bill. He even got Ted Kennedy, the alleged murdering Socialist Senator from Massachusetts, to go along with him. "No Child Left Behind" may not be the total answer to our educational woes, but it is a structured start to try and provide measure and guidance.

Here is my finish: Less than 38% of the working population has a college degree. By the year 2010, it is predicted that one in five high school youth will be a Hispanic. Their scores on the SAT are well below both blacks and whites. Barely 50% of the Hispanics have a high school diploma, compared to 84% of the total population. A hideously low 10% of the Hispanics have college degrees, compared to 26% of the total population. The gap is expected to widen in the next ten years, begging the question: Where does that leave us in ten years?

CHAPTER TWELVE

DON'T BE WILLFULLY IGNORANT

TO ENJOY LIVING and, hopefully, having a long and productive life, I have some suggestions that may be of help to you. First, I'd give myself time to get going in the morning. Yeah, I know those of you with children will have a difficult time finding those extra minutes, but, at least, consider it.

I have slightly modified my morning ritual, and it was likely a big factor in my loss of 15-20 pounds. I have a tasty Bran cereal called Honey Clusters in orange juice (due to lactose intolerance) with Vitamin D and calcium, good glass of water and a banana. It will keep you going for a few hours. Instead of coffee, which I came to tolerate after giving up Coke, I have now switched to caffeine capsules, which do the "boost" trick. While eating, I read the newspaper, usually USA Today, or a local paper on the weekend. The paper, along with the Internet, keeps me informed about the news of the world. In this day and time, with people like "Slick Willie", the "Reverends", and the "towel heads" around, it is vital to be aware of the "affairs" of the world. Regular reading makes life more interesting and allows you to filter through media prejudices to form your personal opinions and make well-informed decisions in all facets of life, particularly in voting. Otherwise, you easily become one of the 30% of the U.S. population considered "willfully ignorant," according to my gal, the great author and conservative leader Ann Coulter.

After eating, and usually before a shower, I visit the bathroom for what my Dad called his "daily constitutional." I recommend more reading during this process of "clearing." I also call it "Plus Seven," as my theory is that your IQ increases by a minimum of seven points after completion of the "clearing."

So, before you even leave the house, you're better informed and smarter. Wait, I'm not finished. As you will read in the "Relationships" chapter, I basically overworked myself into allergy problems during the middle to late 1980's. I went through allergy shots for four years and improved marginally. Along the way, I also took various prescription and over-the-counter drugs. Whenever I would find one that would ease the allergy-induced symptoms, it would gradually lose its effectiveness. Along the way, I took the prescription drugs Seldane and Hismanal, sometimes in unison. These two were later declared dangerous as a combination, apparently the cause of numerous heart attacks. Glad I survived, but the Seldane did cause me to have a mild case of Al Gore's punctured ozone layer on top of my head.

After four years of allergy shots, I decided to pursue other options for allergy relief. I was not willing to accept the fact that I would have to live with the allergies for the remainder of my life. My younger sister, a thin jogger and former wellness coordinator of a hospital, had spurred my interest in health literature. I read several stories about the use of natural substances and decided to get a catalog from one of the advertised companies. The list of products included "Allergy First Aid", "Endless Energy", and "Natural Breathing". The focus of these products seemed to be perfect for my allergy symptoms and they were exactly so. My symptoms disappeared nearly overnight and have not returned. For all you sufferers, I hope this information might be of help to you. I have added a few more herbs and minerals, along with specific supplements with targeted purposes.

On the way to work, I recommend listening to your favorite music to help you arrive in a better frame of mind. TV advertisements are now stating that singing can add significant years to your life, easing anxiety and lowering blood pressure and heart rate. At some point during the day, I hope you will find the opportunity for some form of exercise. The evidence continues to mount that regular exercise is absolutely essential for mental and physical well-being. Take your kids or spouse with you, but do it. The exercise will likely mean more opportunities for "clearing" and getting those seven points on the IQ scale, among many other benefits.

CHAPTER THIRTEEN

GET OFF YOUR ASS AND DO SOMETHING

"THE FIRST WEALTH is health"-Ralph Waldo Emerson

Evidence is growing that inactive people can improve their health by starting a regular exercise program at a moderate intensity level. Let's begin with the children and the ugly trends. During the last 25 years, the proportion of overweight kids ages 6 to 11 more than doubled, while overweight in adolescents tripled.

Some 18 percent of all school-age children are now overweight. Because of this, these young people face an increased risk for adult heart disease, diabetes, and other illnesses for life. The physical activity rates for our youth are terrible, with just 25% of high school age children engaging at a moderate rate of 30 minutes a day, five days a week. National Dietary Guidelines recommend that children get an hour of daily exercise, so even the 25% are only getting half of the suggested activity rate.

The schools are not helping. Daily participation in high school physical education dropped from 42% in 1991 to 33% in 2005. Ten percent of high school students did not participate in **any** moderate or vigorous physical activity in 2005.

According to a study from my alma mater, UNC-Chapel Hill, adolescent obesity has increased significantly among second and third generation immigrants to the United States. Barry Popkin, professor of nutrition at UNC, notes that "the risk of hypertension and diabetes among adolescents is increasing rapidly, and both these diseases are strongly associated with being overweight. Adolescent obesity often leads to adult obesity and a large number of health problems are linked with adult obesity". Of the nearly 14,000 adolescents from the nationally representative sample, 26.5% were obese. Individual rates are: non-Hispanic whites, 24.2%; black non-Hispanics, 30.9%; all Hispanics 30.4% and all Asian-Americans 20.6%. Not surprisingly to me, black females, at 34%, were the only female-group with higher rates than males.

The presence of family is also significant in helping protect adolescents from obesity. The Add Health Study reported that strong and supportive ties between parents and children were found to help protect adolescents against a variety of risky behaviors, including substance abuse, early sexual activity, emotional distress and violence. Obviously, the future does not look bright when so many of our children are on the wrong road for a happy, healthy adult life.

Despite the proven benefits of physical activity, more than half of American adults do not get enough exercise to provide health benefits. Twenty-five percent of adults are totally inactive in their leisure time, and activity decreases with age.

According to the Center for Disease Control (CDC), regular physical activity can improve health and reduce the risk of premature death in the following ways:

1. Reduces the risk of developing coronary heart disease (CHD) and the risk of dying from CHD.
2. Reduces the risk of stroke.
3. Reduces the risk of having a second heart attack in people who have already had one heart attack.
4. Lowers both total blood cholesterol and triglycerides and increases high-density lipoproteins (HDL) or the "good" cholesterol.
5. Lowers the risk of developing high blood pressure.
6. Helps reduce blood pressure in people who already have hypertension.
7. Lowers the risk of developing non-insulin-dependent (type 2) diabetes mellitus.
8. Reduces the risk of developing colon cancer.
9. Helps people achieve and maintain a healthy body weight.

10. Reduces feelings of depression and anxiety.

11. Promotes psychological well-being and reduces feelings of stress.

12. Helps build and maintain healthy bones, muscles, and joints.

13. Helps older adults become stronger and better able to move about without falling or becoming excessively fatigued.

The issue of exercise is very important to me. I have seen too many people damage their bodies and minds by not being properly active. It can be damaging to relationships, believe me from personal experience, and, more importantly, to long-term health. Millions of overweight baby boomers are on track to becoming disabled senior citizens. The longer a person has been obese, the greater wear on joints and the probability of developing type 2 diabetes, according to Richard Suzman of the National Institute of Aging. Type 2 is *bad*, as it can lead to blindness, kidney failure, amputations, heart attacks and stroke. Diabetes hammers not just the body, but the mind. As blood sugar control worsens, the Alzheimer's risk rises quickly. Cells start to starve in type 2 diabetes.

By 2030, after all the baby boomers have turned 65, there will be 71 million senior citizens in the USA. At present, according to the CDC and Prevention magazine, one-third of the U.S. adult population is obese. There has been a dramatic rise in the number of disabilities in the 30-50 year old age group over the last 20 years. The rise in disabilities is likely to increase future nursing home populations, putting a further strain on the health care industry. There were 52,000 nursing assistant vacancies in 2006. With health care costs already growing dramatically, the prospects for elder care are downright frightening. The best course of action is to work to avoid those extra medical costs.

Fidelity Investments estimates that a couple retiring now will need $200,000 to cover health costs over a 15 year period, with prescription drugs making up a third of the cost. The calculation does not include dental costs, long-term care, or over-the-counter medications. Diabetes per-capita health care is estimated to be 2.4 times higher than those without the disease. The "Annals of Internal Medicine" reports that 15-30 minutes of exercise a day reduces the chance of dementia by 30-40%, and elevated blood pressure and heart disease risk is cut substantially.

Lastly, and more personally for me, is the mental benefit of exercise. In a N.Y. Times op-ed column from November 8, 2007, Sandra Aamodt and Sam Wong, in a piece headed "Exercise on the Brain," they reported that physical exercise has been shown to maintain and improve brain health. "In humans, exercise improves what scientists call "executive function," the set of abilities that allows you to select behavior that's appropriate to the situation, inhibit inappropriate behavior and focus on the job at hand in spite of distractions. Executive function includes basic functions like processing speed, response speed and working *memory*, the type used to remember a house number while walking from the car to a party."

"Executive function starts to decline when people reach their 70's. But elderly people who have been athletic all their lives have much better executive function than sedentary people of the same age. When inactive people get more exercise, even starting in their 70's, their executive function improves, as shown in a recent meta-analysis of 18 studies."

"Exercise is also strongly associated with a reduced risk of **dementia** late in life. People who exercise regularly in middle-age are *one-third* as likely to get **Alzheimer's disease** in their 70's as those who did not exercise. Even people who begin exercising in their 60's have their risk reduced by half."

Aamont, editor in chief of "Nature Neoscience", and Wang, associate professor of molecular biology and neuroscience at Princeton, conclude their editorial with a very sound piece of advice. "Instead of spending money on computer games or puzzles to improve your brain's health, invest in a gym membership. Or, just turn off the computer and go for a brisk walk."

Aamont and Wang are authors of a new book titled "Welcome to Your Brain: Why You Lose Your Car Keys but Never Forget How to Drive and Other Puzzles of Everyday Life." I wish them great success, sounds most interesting.

WHY NOT START THEM EARLY?

If you don't have the personal discipline for exercise, at least give your kids a chance. Fitness classes for children as young as three months are becoming available. A chain called "My Gym Children Fitness Center" now has nearly 200 locations nationwide, as well as in Turkey, Mexico and France, among others. With an age range of three months to nine years, the chain offers a variety of activities.

I applaud the efforts of schools in Pennsylvania and Florida. After screenings, letters are being sent home to parents whose children are considered to have a weight problem. The letters encourage parents to change their child's eating habits and help them get more exercise.

Need some evidence to help you make that decision to guide your children to a more active life? At the Medical College of Georgia, sedentary, overweight kids from seven to eleven years old were put on an aerobic fitness plan. The kids lost one to two percent of their body fat, and brain scans found that there was more neural activity in the frontal areas of their brains. Darla Castelli, Assistant Professor of Kinesiology and Community Health at Illinois-Urbana-Champaign, said "This research corroborates several of our studies, which also examined executive function in kids. We found strong association between math performance and aerobic fitness among elementary school age children."

Another new study confirmed that exercise builds strong brains. It showed that children exercising 20-40 minutes a day may be better able to organize schoolwork, class projects, and learn math. The findings showed that the children in the 40 minute group had significant improvement on an executive function test compared with a control group, and the 20 minute group had half as much improvement.

The numbers don't lie. The average weight of kids 6-11 years old was 65 in 1966, but had jumped to 74 by 2002. Boys aged 12-17 were an average of 125 pounds in 1966, but that number is up to 141 for 2002. The girls went from 118 to 130 pounds in the same time period.

That was me (the author) in April 2006 after ear surgery (back cover).

CHAPTER FOURTEEN

THE BEST AND WORST
OF TELEVISION

I'M GOING TO call myself an expert on television, as I do watch it quite a bit, particularly during baseball season. I also enjoy a few regular shows, many movies, and, more recently, a few talk shows. At home and at a vacation home, I subscribed to cable and satellite. While I am not fond of cable (or other monopolies), it is helpful for picture-in-picture to be able to watch two channels at once.

Another advantage of having both cable and satellite is to avoid commercials. Most are insulting, like phone company ads. Paul Reiser made a fool of himself in his ads, missing his effective humorous style by a mile. Now we have the stupid "Can you hear me now?" Lastly, "Carrot Top" might be the most obnoxious person on television.

These ad companies get paid well. Why can they not be more creative? Most products are known to people, so the goal would seem to be to create a "catchy" idea or attachment. Examples that worked are the Budweiser frogs and, to a lesser extent, the lizards. The Bud Lite ladies commercials were also appealing because of humor. Miller has made a comeback with the beer delivery man who actually takes High Life beer **out** of a restaurant because the eatery has high prices. Some favorites from the past are the "Dow Scrubbing Bubbles" from the Dow Bathroom Cleaner, which go scooting around the tub working extra hard, so you don't have toooooooooooo-as they disappear down the drain. Another from Miller was the celebrity commercial headed by the late Rodney Dangerfield, as usual getting "no respect" from others.

While many of the network primetime shows are easily avoided, there have been and still are a few to recommend. Syndication is a welcome facet of television, as is the release of archive DVD's. "Hawaii 5-0" (1968-1980), with Jack Lord as Steve McGarrett, was a great attraction, particularly when he would get pissed off during an episode. "Mr. Ed," the black and white show about a talking horse, had many excellent showings, particularly when Ed tried out with the L.A. Dodgers and slid into home. The same was true for the "Munsters," when Herman had a tryout and knocked a player backwards with a throw. "Soap," a comedy in the late 1970's, was a controversial show that included Billy

Crystal as a homosexual. There was also his brother, who carried a ventriloquist dummy with him. Whether the creators know it or not, it seems to me that the influences of both "Soap" and the shows "Monty Python's Flying Circus" and the short running "Police Squad" series are in the animated comedy classic "South Park" series.

It is very pleasing to see "South Park" ignore the "politically correct" arena. "Blazing Saddles," the movie by Mel Brooks in the late 70's, made a joke about nearly everyone, but that seemed to be the end of the "politically incorrect" productions. Whoever coined the term of politically incorrect, as Cartman would respond, "sucks ass". "PC" has only served to alienate more people, often improperly define others and maintain a level of tension among various groups of people. It is basically an "ism", a label frequently used as a weak defense. "South Park" holds nothing back and takes the attitude that no subject or individual is immune to ridicule. Humor is an effective ingredient against tension. People need to lighten up or the world will have little success in breaking down the multiple barriers. Race, for example, is one of these areas. Chris Rock, successful black comedian, has expressed a most appropriate approach to the biggest racial question. He says we must get past the use of the "N" word. In an interview with Ed Bradley of "60 Minutes," Rock was questioned about his use of the word. "This country is fascinated by anything a white man can't do, like say that word. The whole "nigger" thing is blown out of proportion. Don't people have other things to do? Clean up the crack house, find a cure for something.....Racisms hysterical, the attitudes are funny, but the effects are horrible. A lot of ignorance is funny. We laugh at the dumb guy, at Woody on "Cheers." When you laugh at it, you forget about it."

As Joe Pesci, his co-star in the movie "Lethal Weapon 4," puts it "People laugh at the logic of his humor-at the people who live off welfare, don't work, think they're cool because they go to jail, think people who graduate from college as sissies. He doesn't have to be militant about it, and he does the same thing with the white people. He's got both sides covered." For example, Rock on being bused to a poor white neighborhood: "Ain't nothing scarier than poor white people. Even white people are scared of poor white people. They lived under the trailer home. They weren't white trash; they were white toxic waste."

Rock also addressed the use of profanity, which is used effectively in "South Park," particularly by Eric Cartman. "Vulgar? Obscene? Who makes these rules? It's OK to show Don Johnson shoot someone on "Miami Vice" or Schwarzenegger kill a bunch of people in the movies, but if I say (foul language) that's vulgar? I get asked about this all the time, and I'm like: You ignorant people, grow up. Cursing is used for emphasis; it's never the joke."

Chris, now that you have been recognized by your peers as a terrific comedian, I hope even more people will listen to the message in your work. It is time for our country to open its mind on many subjects and race is perhaps highest on the list. There will be no real progress in race relations until we can get to that point.

I first viewed "South Park" in February, 1998, after it had aired about five episodes. "Pink Eye" was the episode title and it was focused on Halloween. The four main characters dressed up for a school Halloween costume contest. Two as Chewbacca, the loveable lion-human type of animal from the Star Wars movies, one as Raggedy Andy because of his girlfriend, and Cartman as Hitler. After arriving at school, Cartman is whisked off to view a sensitivity tape, but he is more impressed by the fact the people were saluting the Fuehrer. Despite his objections, the school principal insisted that the costume be changed and did so by putting a white sheet over him. You can see where this is going. The boys then go trick or treating and they visit the home of Chef, the black school cook. The white sheet wasn't happily received, but the eight-year old boys did not know any better, and it was hilarious.

Other subjects and individuals that have been ridiculed by "South Park" are lesbianism, homosexuality, starvation, injured war veterans, poor people, talk shows, education, disfigurement, hate crimes, the handicapped and Barbara Streisand (rightfully so), Fred Savage, Kathy Lee Gifford, Tom Hanks, Sally Strothers, Janet Reno (big-time), Hillary and Bill Clinton, Al Gore and Robert Redford. From what I have read, only Streisand (no big surprise) has been sufficiently offended to consider retaliation, although Tom Cruise also had some issues.

While I don't recommend "South Park" to young kids because of the language, I do hope it will help contribute to a relaxation of sensitivity to numerous subject matters. Maintaining the present levels of tension on race, gays, ignorance and others will only mean more difficult problems for the future.

The present television shows for recommendation are "Boston Legal," with the classic team of James Spader and William Shatner, "CSI Miami" (David Caruso with a nice comeback), "Curb Your Enthusiasm" (hope Larry David keeps doing it), "24" (hope someone will find Keifer Sutherland a driver), "Men in Trees" (brilliant job by gay-reformed Anne Heche), "Numbers", "Grey's Anatomy", "Prison Break", "Bones" and "House" (Hugh Laurie is great). These shows fit no particular mold, are not afraid to tackle sensitive subjects or use significant creativity in their subject matter. I think "Hill Street Blues" was a great leader in the trend of shows more closely mirroring real life.

I have to save the best for last. Where would we be without ESPN? I remember the early days and am very appreciative that they persevered while continuing a dedication to quality. It is more than refreshing to see that ESPN has not taken itself too seriously, often playfully mocking itself and its "Sports Center" anchor people. Also, being a huge baseball fan, I thoroughly enjoy "Baseball Tonight." Anyway, great job to Chris, Dan, Keith (when he was there; he sucks on MSNBC), and all the others for their excellent work, and please keep having fun.

CHAPTER FIFTEEN

MUSIC-
WHO MADE IT,
WHO RUINED IT

WHILE MY MUSICAL favorites are The Beatles and Paul McCartney, the record buying public also has clearly stated the same choice. The Beatles have the most No.1 hits of anyone and can anyone ever match having the number one through number five on the single charts as they did in 1964? The Anthology Series, released in November of 1996, began a string of three double CD's for the group. Each debuted at number one, a remarkable achievement considering the group disbanded in 1970, largely due to Yoko Ono and, to some degree, John Lennon. Of the three CD's, there was only six totally unreleased songs, which included two new ("Free As A Bird" and "Real Love") recordings completed by Paul, George and Ringo that had been started as home demos by John from the 1970's. Nevertheless, it was fascinating to hear the song development process presented on the CD's and interesting to note that the group universally managed to mold their songs to the best possible form. Even the old Beatle songs are best-sellers, evidenced by the "1" CD, a compilation of chart-toppers by the group released in 2000. "1" topped the charts in 34 countries and will likely become the best-selling album of all time. Up to date numbers show 170 million albums sold by The Beatles, with Garth Brooks a distant second at 123 million, just ahead of Elvis Presley.

The best music has "staying power," where certainly The Beatles are the prime example. Even the solo Beatles have done remarkably well, with Paul being the most consistently successful, beginning with "McCartney" in 1970, released about the same time as The Beatles last album, "Let It Be," until his last two outstanding releases titled "Chaos and Creation in the Backyard" and "Memory Almost Full." While George often seemed to be casting out demons from his tortured recollection of The Beatles, he produced excellent work such as "All Things Must Pass" from the early 1970's, "Cloud Nine" from the late 80's and his last album "Brainwashed" in 2002, released the year after his death. Ringo, perhaps underrated for his talent, has done some excellent recent work as well, such as "Vertical Man," "Choose Love," and "Liverpool 8."

Other artists with staying power are The Rolling Stones, The Who, Elton John, Billy Joel, and Bruce Springsteen. To a lesser extent, The Temptations and Four Tops music has also endured. Brian Wilson and Stevie Wonder are two individuals that are great songwriters and musical talents. I know there are others, but their music is not that appealing to me, so write your own book.

The beauty of The Beatles was their desire not to repeat themselves. Examine their change from "Rubber Soul" to "Revolver" to "Sgt. Peppers" to "The White Album" and through "Abbey Road". The death of their manager, Brian Epstein, was certainly an unsettling influence on the group, creating the need for the young artists, all in their 20's, to monitor their business dealings. They had no training to do so, and it affected the chemistry of the group. It has to be difficult to argue about matters where there was little basic understanding. More importantly, the unsettled childhood of John Lennon and the influence of a shrieking Yang (negative definition for a Japanese) named Yoko were the main factors behind the breakup of the group. As noted in the development of many gays, and the continued cycle of despair for blacks, the family life and childhood are the major influences on the behavioral patterns of adults. John had a completely absent father and nearly absent mother named Julia, an apparently delightful person. Raised by his Aunt Mimi, John was troubled from the beginning and then his mother, whom he seemed to love dearly, was killed by an automobile driven by a drunken policeman. These factors helped create a hard edge in the personality of John. While this edge was not always a negative, as apparent in his contributions to The Beatles, the heroin habit of the late 60's combined with the hard edge to create a highly volatile Lennon. The other Beatles walked on eggshells in 1968 while recording "The White Album," not knowing which side of John they would face at any given moment. This in itself had to begin destroying the chemistry, but consider that John had brought Yoko into the recording studio, previously the domain of the band members, producer George Martin and assistant Mal Evans. Bringing her to the studio was bad enough, but Yoko had the unbelievable gall to make musical suggestions to the group. In his book, "Two of Us," by Geoffrey Guiliano, the author of several books about the Beatles, a recording session employee recalled the interference of Yoko. "I remember she turned to Paul and said, "Why don't we try it this way?" Paul exploded and asked John: "What the hell is going on? We never had anyone in the studio before. Why have we suddenly got somebody interfering with our work? Either she goes or I go." John said, "She's not going," and Paul stormed out. "It was about a week before they could get Paul back into the studio. That was the beginning of the serious friction."

"Most galling of all," revealed Beatle friend Pete Shotten, "Yoko felt little hesitation about offering her own criticisms of their work", about which, of course, she knew next to nothing. This was bad enough, but recent reports have indicated that John was interested in writing again with Paul in 1980. This was reported by the producer of the last complete Lennon album, "Double Fantasy." Jack Douglas indicated that John was awaiting word from Paul regarding their reunion, but Yoko blocked any calls from reaching John. Douglas also had to fight Yoko over the royalties from the album. Sensing perhaps that she would be remembered as a main ingredient in the group separation, Yoko was gracious (or greedy) enough to provide the "Threatles" (Paul, George and Ringo) with John's demo tape of a few songs. Yoko, of course, would also share in the proceeds of the tapes that would become a part of The Beatles Anthology. John, we all miss you, but pity the fact that you brought the meddling Yang into the sanctity of the greatest musical group of all time.

From the best to worst. Rap music. Devoid on melody, the lyrics have grown from bad to outright criminal. The bass, often the only part of the music you can hear in rap, usually just rattles your teeth. If you want to hear the best bass playing, listen to the Beatles "Rain" and "Something," and "My Brave Face" by McCartney. Since the words of some of the rap music are so abusive, they should not be available for purchase by children.

I have to include one letter regarding "Hip Hop", or whatever they want to call this crap now.

"This style of urban music openly demeans women, turning them into nothing more than sexual play toys, boasts of drug use and violence, brags about how they survived during their illegal exploits; and uses a plethora of four letter words that now pervade the language of kids as young as eight or nine years old.

Instead of turning off people by touting their sexual exploits, alcohol and drug usage, the coolness of even elementary school kids dropping F-bombs everywhere, violence and heroes who died violently while promoting this "music", these artists could have opened the eyes of society to the injection and the blight of the deteriorating inner cities."

DAVE FULTON-Sarasota, FL

The record companies ought to take the lead and refuse to release the product. It was a shame to see the followers of black music go from the melodious music of Motown to the rap crap and incessant wailing of singers (?) like the arrogant and addicted Whitney Houston. Why was she allowed to walk away from police in Hawaii after they found pot in her baggage? Nice attitude, Whitney and nice former husband. How many times has he been arrested?

Country music has made some nice changes, going from mostly the twang style to a broader range of sound. Personally, I enjoy the soft rock influence, particularly that of Garth Brooks and Mary Chapin Carpenter. I have not seen Garth in concert, but everyone that I know who has done so has thoroughly enjoyed it. The song "To Make You Feel My Love" by Garth for the movie, "Hope Floats" is a nice touch.

Preferring the song writing genius of the Beatles, I find the practice of recording previously done songs to be seriously lacking, especially since those re-recording Beatles' songs are most often a butcher job. While discussing music, let me tell you about an ultra-talented group called the Spongetones. The Sponge part was derived from the group's admiration of the Beatles as they "sponged" off the songs and style of the Fab Four. I was fortunate enough to book the band in October of 1999 for a high school reunion, and it was an outstanding performance. While able to play many Beatle songs and other music from the 60's and 70's to near perfection, the group has recorded a number of original songs with a classic style of their own. Yeah, go out and try to find their CD's or let me know if you need help locating their recordings.

Being from North Carolina and loving the beach, it would seem natural that I would enjoy "beach music." For some reason, the act of dancing in some structured fashion never appealed to me. Some of the music was tolerable, but a majority was not. Being in Chapel Hill as a youth, we were exposed to a changing world earlier and beach music was not a significant part of our culture. Therefore, when going to school at Carolina, I was quite surprised to be exposed to an avalanche of beach music at the fraternity where I became a member. The dormitory where I spent my freshman year was more in tune with the music of the day, Stones, Who, Zeppelin, etc.

I saved the worst for last. Michael Jackson. Did he fondle the kids? His career was near ruin until Paul McCartney was kind enough to collaborate on a few songs. "Say Say Say" was tolerable, but

"The Girl is Mine" was a low point for Paul. The collaboration brought Jackson back into the limelight as Paul had been on a successful run, just having the number one album in "Tug of War." While working with Paul, Michael quizzed him about ideas for investing. Paul suggested music publishing. Michael kidded Paul that he might someday buy the rights to the Beatles' songs, something that should have been owned by the group from the very beginning. Ironically, the rights to the songs became available several years later. Paul called Yoko, a thoughtful gesture, and suggested that it would take at least $20 million each to buy the rights. The Yang, being the musical expert that she is, thought that she and Paul could get the rights at a cheaper price, and should wait out the bidding. Jackson, forgetting his assistance from Paul and flush with cash from the "Bad" album, bid $47 million for the rights without having the courtesy of calling Paul. He has since cheapened the songs by allowing them to be used on TV commercials, an idea the Beatles had rejected completely, despite many lucrative offers. Thanks, Yoko, whose son Sean has made negative remarks about Beatle fans, and thanks, Michael. Jackson's character is obviously flawed and his career appears done. We all know why he had to leave the United States. Good riddance.

If you think I have been too hard on Yoko, let me present you with a few lines from Mike Douglas and his autobiography. John and Yoko appeared on the Douglas show during a week in 1972. "No one was ever harder for our staff to please (than Yoko). Yoko wanted it warmer. Yoko wanted it colder. Yoko said there wasn't enough of a certain color in the dressing room. Yoko wanted it quieter. Yoko wanted it louder. Yoko wanted it brighter. Yoko wanted it darker. Another week and Yoko wouldn't be just responsible for breaking up the Beatles, she'd break up The Mike Douglas Show, too."

Let's put the martyr stuff aside. Yoko and John were the major cause of the breakup of the Beatles.

THE BEST OF ALL TIME

I have seen Paul McCartney in concert 22 times. In 2002, I saw him four times in six days. With the unbelievable assistance of old friends, I was able to secure excellent seats, including second row on the floor in Fort Lauderdale, directly in front of Paul. The shows were classics, consisting of 21 Beatle songs, and 15 other excellent McCartney songs. The middle third of the show consisted of a mostly solo set by Paul, an ultimate treat for the serious fan. For over two and a half hours, the crowd was entertained with some of the best music of the last forty years. McCartney, and his mostly youthful band, were greeted by highly enthusiastic crowds, a well-deserved response for the greatest artist of all time.

One of the reasons for the breakup of the Beatles cited by many observers was disputes about the "Let it Be" album. Not completely satisfied with the initial recordings, John led the charge to get crazy Phil Spector to "finish" the album. Phil was known for his "wall of sound," which may have helped some artists with their recordings, but not the Beatles. Especially galling were the strings and ladies voices added to "The Long and Winding Road," a beautiful song in original form. The pressure within the group had built during the making of the album, as Paul tried to coax the group into performing live again. He did his best to keep things together, trying to lead while respecting his beloved group members. Having already lost the battle on hiring a new manager, Allan Klein, a decision the others would regret, Paul could not accept the Spector ruination of his song.

In late 2003, **Let it Be**….**Naked** was released. It was the album in the form that Paul wanted. Ringo, despite all of the earlier trouble with the original release, openly agreed that Paul had been right about the album. "You're bloody right again, it sounds great without Phil."

CHAPTER SIXTEEN

IDOLS AND ASSHOLES

I DO NOT THINK it is necessary to idolize anyone. Role model seems a little weak to adequately describe the strengths and weaknesses of the people highlighted in this chapter. I can't include everyone in this one chapter, but decided to start with those that I found the most interesting and offensive. For the assholes, you have earned your title, and if I write a follow up to this book, there will certainly be more to add to the list.

First on my list is Arnold Palmer. His way of playing the game of golf is nearly enough by itself. The attacking, go for broke style exploded golf onto the national scene. In 1960, Arnie, as he is known to most, birdied the last two holes at Augusta to win the Masters by one shot. A few months later, seven shots back with 18 holes left, Arnie drove the green on the par four first hole, shot 30 on the front nine and finished with a round of 65 to win the U.S. Open by two strokes. His talent was obvious, but his persona was overwhelming. Always aware and appreciative of the crowd, Arnie's followers became "Arnie's Army." They shared in his infamous charges as he shot up the scoreboard on the final day of the tournament and agonized with him as the PGA Championship eluded Palmer, keeping him from being one of a handful of golfers to win golf's proverbial "Grand Slam," which is made up of all four of the major professional championships (Masters, U.S. Open, PGA, and British Open). He came close several times in the PGA, but perhaps the darkest moment in Arnie's career came in the 1966 U.S. Open. Leading by seven strokes with just nine holes left remaining, Arnie kept attacking, shooting to break the Open scoring record. Billy Casper, basically playing for second place, quietly shot a 32 while Arnie had a 39 on the last nine. In the playoff the next day, Arnie again led early, only to lose the lead. It was one of the darkest moments in sports history. The 1964 Masters would be the last major championship Arnie would win on the PGA Tour. Even in his darkest moments, Arnie would always exhibit an air of class and sportsmanship. It would have been beneficial to golfers of today if Arnie's domination of the tour had come during the last 20 years of the golden age of television.

Nevertheless, listen to his fellow competitors on the Senior Tour. "He's the ultimate superstar, and we've been lucky to have him. Anytime he plays, it means a lot to the game. If there's ever been a person synonymous with anything, it's Arnold Palmer in golf. He's our hero; he's certainly mine." This is from Ray Floyd. Jim Colbert, another successful senior player, credits Arnie with bringing golf into the modern era. "He's our Babe Ruth. He's brought the senior circuit to where it is today. Our whole show today has been built on what Arnold did, with the start of TV coverage and right up to the modern day." In perhaps my greatest sports thrill, I had the privilege of walking the eighteen holes of Latrobe Country Club with Arnie in September of 1999. He was playing in a tournament of local amateurs and club pros. It was not publicized, but a good friend's in-laws lived in the area and knew Arnie a little through his brother. Their son, John, an excellent golfer in his own right, was also playing in the tournament. Before the tournament, I was introduced to Arnie and his long-time assistant, "Doc" Giffin. I had brought some old magazines from the 50's that featured Arnie on the cover and offered to give them to him. He asked "Doc" if they already had the magazines and the answer was affirmative. Arnie then offered to sign them for me, which was not my intention. He graciously signed them, and then started to progress toward the first tee. I was able to walk the entire eighteen holes talking to Arnie whenever the time seemed right. We talked about clubs, (I use Palmer equipment), football, and designing golf courses. Carolina had already played one football game that year, losing on a last-minute field goal to Virginia. Having attended Wake Forest, Arnie got in the dig that our football team was not very good. I couldn't disagree, and his school also beat us that year, as the last game of a seven game losing streak for Carolina. Arnie knew his football, as Carolina finished 3-8. The whole day was like catching up with a great old friend. Thanks, Arnie and there will never be another golfer like you.

While most "real" golfers have adopted Arnie's style and pace of play, too many have seen Jack Nicklaus and his deliberate approach to the game. While grudgingly accepting that Jack has accomplished more on the course than any golfer-to date, I am repelled by his style of play and lack of graciousness. I had a first-hand look at Arnie and Jack at the famous No. 2 course in Pinehurst, site of the 1999 and 2005 Men's U.S. Opens. Arnie and Jack played an exhibition match for the revived Shell's Wonderful World of Golf at No. 2 on April 12, 1994. Yelling for Arnie on every shot, I was thrilled to have the chance to see him up close with the opportunity to pay Jack back for the '62 and '67 Opens, and just for taking the limelight away from the greatest man in golf. The match was close for awhile, but Jack got a few lucky breaks and pulled ahead later in the round. One hole, however, would capture the difference between Jack and Arnie. On the 15th hole, a relatively long par three, Jack hit a long iron, which hit near the back of the green and rolled over. He turned to his caddie in disbelief saying "I can't believe that green wouldn't hold that ball. What is wrong with these greens?" Stunned that he would make that comment in front of a mostly local crowd that takes pride in their beautiful course, I walked down the fairway discussing the Nicklaus comment with my friend from work. One of the locals overheard my remarks of disgust and responded by saying, "It doesn't matter, 99 percent of the people here are for Arnie anyway." Case closed.

I have to add a little more. Jack's golf courses seem to be built with complete disdain for the average golfer. The Rams Club at Carolina sponsored about 8-10 golf tournaments per year the last several years I worked there, and we made every effort to avoid any Nicklaus courses. We played one on our 1998 Rams Club "Mini-Tour" in Pinehurst and despite my enjoyable playing partners, I was completely put off by the "tricked-up" holes and unfair greens. After the round, we were fortunate to have our post-tournament function at the Pinecrest Inn, an absolutely delightful place with one of the best bars in the country. The staff is excellent and you can sing with a piano player on Saturday nights, but it helps to know the words of the songs being played.

Walking into the Pinecrest that day, I passed a childhood friend that had played in the tournament. I asked him what he thought about the golf course. "Jack Nicklaus should start designing tennis courts" was his reply. I had given Jack the benefit of the doubt only because of my visit to Muirfield Village in Dublin, Ohio, site of the PGA's Memorial Tournament. It was an enjoyable, challenging course. However, a few years ago, I was playing golf in the Myrtle Beach area with a dedicated golfer who was then partner in five golf courses of the "Grand Strand." We were discussing Jack and his golf courses before the conversation got more personal. "I've never known anyone who liked Jack" was his first response. After I stated that I thought Muirfield Village was a good course, I was informed that my playing partner had met the man who claimed credit for the design of Muirfield. It wasn't Jack, but he had a definitive opinion of Jack. "The biggest asshole I have met in my life."

Lastly, Jack's style of play has seriously damaged golf in another way. His deliberate "plays it safe" style has created clones that play badly and take too long. Anyone using visualization on the golf course needs to stay home or play another sport.

I want to move back to the positive side and start by saying that Jack Nicklaus II went to school at Carolina and I found him to be both humble and personable. Good job, Barbara (his Mom).

At Carolina, we have the Dean. I know he has been out of coaching since 1997, but thank goodness he is still around and Roy Williams is now the head coach. I am glad Coach Smith retired, because it gave him more time to do other things he likes to do, such as playing good golf. Coach Smith gave Carolina nearly 40 years of his working life, and has remained available for players and coaches. When he started in Chapel Hill in 1960, the basketball program had taken a downward turn, even though there was an undefeated national championship year in 1957. After taking over as coach in 1962, the basketball program started a gradual improvement before exploding to three straight Final Fours from 1967-1969. Another Final Four in 1972 was perhaps a lost opportunity as Carolina fell to Florida State in the semi-finals. I do not like to make excuses, but with Carolina rallying, Bob McAdoo was called for his fifth foul with inside position on a rebound. Five years later, the finals were in Atlanta. After spectacular wins over Kentucky and Notre Dame in Maryland to get to Atlanta, it appeared the Heels would end their drought of national championships. One of the many great individual game coaching jobs of Coach Smith's career got Carolina past a superior individually talented Nevada-Las Vegas team in the semi-finals, 85-84. Marquette beat UNC-Charlotte in the other semi-final by two points on a highly questionable call on a near length of the court pass. So, it was very, very close to being an all North Carolina final. Carolina went into the final game with the great Phil Ford playing with a hyper-extended elbow, Walter Davis with a broken finger, and having lost their starting center in mid-season. The game started badly, but Carolina made a patented run to tie the game early in the second half, only to lose the momentum. I have always been a bad loser, but this loss was a crusher. It appeared to me there were no dry eyes among the Carolina faithful that day. Coach Smith kept winning games despite these disappointments and returned to the Final Four in 1981 in Philadelphia. This was the school year that I returned to work in Chapel Hill. My wife and I were sitting in a hotel room when the news came that President Reagan and Press Secretary James Brady had been shot in Washington. I cannot adequately describe the feeling, but it was a mixture of deep sorrow and a sense that the world was becoming a more dangerous place. I had wanted Reagan to be the Republican presidential nominee in 1976 and he nearly got it. A fresh face may have given the Republicans a chance to move away faster from the Watergate disaster, as Ford was linked to Nixon because of his pardon of the ex-President. Anyway, instead of Reagan in 1976, we got overmatched Jimmy Carter. I didn't feel like going to a basketball game, and after some apparent discussion to delay the final game, it was played with Indiana winning over Carolina by 63-50. Isiah Thomas led the Hoosiers, but game official Ed Hightower, a Coach Smith nemesis, also hurt the Heels with phantom foul calls on Carolina big men. These comments are not excuses.

Carolina was back in the Final Four in 1982 as I discuss in the "Relationships" chapter. There were again very few dry Carolina eyes, but they were tears of joy this time. Carolina advanced to the finals against Georgetown and the celebration began on Bourbon Street after the one point victory for the Heels. I think even the Coach shed a few tears that night.

There were several great teams after the '82 national championship, like '83, '84 (perhaps the best), '87 and then the 1991 Final Four team, which played in Indianapolis. This was a **nightmare** weekend, beginning with the ticket distribution in the miniscule lobby of an old Holiday Inn converted into a Marriott. Outside the will-call ticket area three hours before the game, Duke University (who was playing Kansas) students began their "Go to hell Carolina, go to hell" chants. At one time, I was always supportive of other teams in the ACC when they played anyone but Carolina. Duke fans cured me of that in 1988 when Duke's team played in the Eastern Regional in the Smith Center. Despite the fact that Carolina was playing in Utah, Duke fans constantly used the same chant in the Smith Center. This began the period when Duke fans openly showed that they derived more pleasure from a Carolina loss than a Duke win. Very sad, because Duke has had great success in basketball since 1991 (winning three national championships), except for the one year of the Valentine's Day team, when their conference record was 2-14. Just as I believe that players often take on the personality of their coach, the same can be said of their fans. I'll get to Coach K later, but let me finish with Coach Smith first.

The Carolina Basketball media guide is filled with stories about the many times that the Heels mounted astounding comebacks from deficits to win games. This ability starts with the leadership and is fueled by competitiveness. Coach Smith fused these traits into an unbelievable career of 879 wins, two national championships, the best record by miles over the conference schools and by graduating nearly all his players. Even when they graduated, they wanted to come back as Coach Smith and his staff provided a deep sense of family for all of the players. Coach Smith always had or made time for a former player, whether he played a little or a lot. This enormous capacity for concern and compassion is only matched by his intelligence. He was constantly one or two steps ahead of his competitors, and ask Duke fans if they know the true reason why Carolina abused them offensively in 1998, if you need any confirmation.

You can also ask Kentucky fans, who have the worst qualities of Duke and N.C. State fans=arrogant rednecks, about the 1995 regional final in Birmingham. Or....I'd have to start another book to list all of these. Call the Carolina Athletic Communications Office if you want more details.

Even though Coach Smith retired from coaching, he remained involved at Carolina. He was also kind enough to continue speaking at Rams Club annual local chapter meetings. I was responsible for a number of these chapters as a function of my job and was fortunate enough to have Coach Smith headlining one of my meetings in the spring of 1998. He arrived after the so-called "cocktail hour," which was his usual practice. I had heard, jokingly, early in my career that he did this to avoid the potential of becoming an alcoholic, as he attended numerous functions. While Coach Smith never said it directly, I believe the functions were a major reason for his retirement. Most of them are at night, and Coach Smith had teenage daughters at the time. This night illustrated another reason. Upon arriving, Coach Smith had numerous requests for autographs for half an hour before we had dinner. After the program, it was autographs again for nearly an hour, as several people came through the line more than once. The autograph hounding is out of control. I did my best to keep the situation under control to little avail and certainly had sympathy for the composed and kind Coach.

Several of Coach's friends, and even the Coach himself, have indicated they thought he would have kept coaching if it were not for the outside commitments. I clearly understand this feeling and the reasons why people abhor the loss of their privacy. Why the hell am I writing this book? Anyway, Coach Smith, many, many thanks for all you have done for Carolina. To those of you who know me personally, yeah, I know I complained about some of our losses in the Smith era. I'll never deny being a bit of a poor loser. Combine that with my feeling for the school and that's a ton of emotion. Losing sucks.

Coach "K." Sorry, his name is too much trouble to spell. We call him the "Cheeseman." When he starts his snarling of profanity at the referees, which is always early in the game, his face closely resembles that of a rat. At the games in Durham, his use of the F-word is constant as he berates the officials on nearly every call, especially in the first half. He also uses the word while addressing the Duke students, telling them before a game with Carolina that if they could not come to the game with "f****ng intensity," then not to show up. At halftime of the 2000 NCAA Tournament game with S.W. Missouri State, one of the opposing team's players stated that he heard the "Cheeseman" screaming "Motherf****r" this and "Mothef****r" that, all through thick concrete walls.

Most officials are intimidated, particularly the ACC's group of referees that are both beholding to Fred Barakat and a less than talented group of game callers. Dick "Dookie" Vitale is always talking about the great job that Barakat did as Coordinator of Officials for the ACC. Wrong. ACC referees have made a number of critical mistakes the last several years and most of the quality officials left the ACC. The finger of blame was often pointed at Barakat. By the way, Fred, where do all the ACC Tournament tickets go that are not allocated to the schools? How well do you know a certain sporting goods representative who always seems to have a large number of tickets, like 125 in recent years? You and the ticket hungry Commissioner must have had some interesting battles about tickets.

Vitale also constantly speaks of the great crowds at Duke's outdated arena. Why? The Duke students cater to his large ego, like passing him up through the crowd, which is ridiculous, and the school made a special presentation to give him a piece of the replaced floor in Cameron. During the last several seasons, many in the media and coaching profession have criticized "Dookie" Vitale for his blatant "rooting" for Duke. The next time your hear Dick spouting off about Duke, think about these reasons. The only quality of the Duke students is enthusiasm. They have long passed any semblance of class in their support. The fight song, only when playing Carolina, has the words "eat shit" sung in it. Personal attacks, both verbal and illustrated, are crude and demeaning. Most Duke students are from the North, which explains part of the problem. They also qualify as great "fair-weather" fans, evidenced after their big choke in the loss to UConn in the 1999 national championship game. Only two fans met the team at the airport upon their return and barely 1,000 attended the season (37-2) celebration at Cameron Indoor.

Coach K provides the balance of classlessness at Duke. He is totally consumed by Carolina, and had great difficulty acknowledging losses to the Heels. Many of his players, such as Christian Laettner, Chris Collins, and the negatively talented "Wojo" took on the Cheeseman's obnoxious personality traits. The most absurd of these examples occurred after another pounding of the Dookies. The game was the last of the regular season and Duke had clinched the regular season title due to a referee's crucial mistake in Duke's game at Virginia. Funny how those "mistakes" usually go in Duke's favor. After the loss to Carolina, the Duke "spin" was that the game was almost meaningless since the regular season title had been decided. This is the biggest rivalry in college basketball. Hey, Dookies and Cheeseman, why not be proud of your success, like the 2001 national championship? It is sad that you derive more pleasure from another team's infrequent losses (except when Matt Doherty was the coach) and this can easily be emotionally damaging. Was Coach K really out with just a back problem during the year when the team went 2-14 in the ACC in 1995; or was it emotional? I'll get back to Coach K in another book.

The arrogance of Coach K, who now has an office on a floor unreachable by the public, has also extended to Duke's (now former) athletic director. In "USA Today", Duke AD Joe Alleva, while discussing the Duke football team, which had gone back-to-back (0-11 seasons, that is) was quoted as saying, "When Florida State came into the conference they raised the bar so high. Now everybody's trying to get there, building new facilities, recommitting to their programs. Most of the ACC (Atlantic Coast

Conference) has a head start on us, but we can offer something nobody else can; a great school." I think that is arguable, Joe.

While we are talking about enjoying another team's losses more than your own successes, let me also say this to N.C. State fans; many of you have the same problem, and Virginia fans holier-than-thou attitude includes a lack of class.

Back to class. Don Mattingly of the New York Yankees. The captain of the team for several years was a quiet leader, whose career was cut short in 1995 by a "real" back injury. Despite the constant pain that developed, "Donnie Baseball," as he was respectfully called by many, rarely complained and did his utmost to bring the Yankees back to stardom. Obviously, they got there with the 1996, 1998-2000 World Series wins and thirteen straight post-season appearances. Many Yankee players gave Don credit for the World Series wins. I do have one complaint about Mattingly; he never sent back my picture of Coach Smith and him in the dugout of Yankee Stadium on opening day of 1994.

I've already mentioned Ronald Reagan. Where would this country be now without him? The "malaise" of Jimmy Carter had left the country in deep trouble. High inflation, a staggering economy, the embarrassing 444 days of Iran's holding of American hostages, and the raging cold war with Russia. Little wonder Carter lost 44 states to Reagan, who immediately took action to revive the economy by across-the-board tax cuts. Defense spending was increased to send a clear message to Russia, the "Evil Empire" as

Reagan would label it. Critics point to the increase in the country's deficit during the Reagan years. Don't forget the legacy of LBJ of wasteful social spending and the fact that the Democrats reneged on a three to one spending cut for tax increases deal agreed to by Reagan. Let's also not forget that the Berlin Wall is gone and Russia was not a threat to the U.S., even being a friend at times, until the recent oil price increase. These changes, a result of Reagan resolve, allowed us to reduce our defense spending as a percentage of the budget until the terrorist's attacks. Unfortunately, the foreign policy success of both the Reagan and Bush, Sr. years was disrupted by appeasement and the pitiful leadership of Clinton. American people, I want you to listen to this (finger pointing at you like Bill did on TV at his "Monica" response), Bill Clinton got way too much credit for the success of the U.S. economy during his tenure. More damaging, by far, is the real story of foreign policy under Clinton. Not responding forcefully after the first World Trade Center bombing to passing on the chance to capture Osama Bin Laden, Bill helped embolden the terrorists.

As Richard Benedetto wrote in "USA Today," the "failure to direct a fair share of Clinton's energy toward foreign affairs may be damaging to what most Presidents consider a President's first responsibility; protecting the national security. The world is a dangerous place." On September 11th, we saw the horror of this fact.

My last choice for "most admired" is actually the greatest individual I have known in my life. You probably did not know him and that's a shame. His name was "Red" Reid. He was the Athletic Ticket Manager at Oklahoma when I came there as an intern from the graduate school at The Ohio State University. He took me under his wing, making me comfortable personally and professionally, allowing me to grow into the job as his assistant and then to replace him as ticket manager. Oklahoma football was "hot" when I arrived and the ticket job had difficult pressure. Despite this, Red kept the staff loose with his always upbeat personality. He was always ready to generate "group discussion" to help ease the pressure and I was a willing participant. Every morning, and often in the afternoon, many people from the ticket and business office staffs would congregate in the lounge area between the two offices. Lively discussions, often triggered by a controversial statement from Red or myself, were the rule of the day. These meetings allowed everyone a break from the time pressures of the job and hopefully the chance to laugh a little. The most remarkable part of this is that Red's personal life had been filled with tragedy. He and his wife had one child, tragically killed early in life while riding a horse. A few years later, while painting a picture of her daughter, his wife suffered a stroke and was an invalid until her death. Red would leave the office three to four times a day to check on his bedridden wife. He rarely would let the ongoing tragedy be an influence on him. On the contrary, he was the shining star of our everyday life. Red, thanks was never enough. Before I leave this, I want to also mention Red's boss, the late Ken Farris. Ken was the Associate Athletic

Director and Business Manager at Oklahoma, and actually the man who offered me the internship. He was serious and soft-spoken, but deeply dedicated to his work. He also took me under his wing, showing me the details of handling team travel as we went to football games away from Norman. I can never forget his many kindnesses and was privileged to be able to work with him. His attention to detail and dedication to the task are two qualities I attempt to implement in my daily work and life. While I was happy to leave Oklahoma to get back to Chapel Hill, I will never forget the guidance, support and friendship extended by Red and Ken, as well as many others that I worked with in Norman.

OTHER TRIBUTES TO ARNIE

Arnie played in his last Masters tournament in April of 2002. Talking with a friend of mine who was there for the week, he told me that the story of the week was Arnie. Even though he had no chance to compete for the title, the crowds were enormous for the 72 year-old Palmer.

At the tournament, Ben Crenshaw said the following: "Everything we have, everything we achieved, is because of the opportunities he gave us. This tournament won't be the same without him." Thanks, Arnie, from all real golfers.

"Palmer was friendly and loved by the fans in spite of his flaws. Nicklaus was aloof and a little too focused on his goals for the fans."-Jerry Potter, USA Today

"He always tried to make us feel better, even when it wasn't apparent that he was feeling badly. Arnie was hugely popular and wealthy, with more demands on his time than any mortal can ever imagine. But, rather than shrink from the public, and his responsibilities, Arnie connected with us on a basic level. With a smile or a wave. Maybe a flirtatious wink. Where would golf be without Arnie? Not even the Masters has a greater legacy than the Master."-Jon Saraceno-USA Today

"There are almost as many Arnold Palmer fans at Augusta National as there are blades of grass.

We see our younger times in Arnold Palmer's eyes. We see our father's faces. As long as he is alive, so are the memories we carry."-Glenn Sheeley-Atlanta Journal Constitution

"Pro golf's family tree started with Arnold Palmer. He carried the PGA on his shoulders for a long time"-Paul Goydos-'96 Bay Hill Invitational winner

"At the 1995 British Open, his last, I needed to escort him from 18 to the media center. It's not a long walk, maybe 100 yards. But we were surrounded by hundreds of fans and the walk took us 90 minutes. He signed autographs for everyone, said hello, looked them in the eye, just talked to every person. I knew then why he was so popular, why he is the King."-Jennifer Mills-Golf Channel broadcast crew original member

SLOW PAY IS COMPARABLE TO
ROOT CANAL

"There is nothing more irritating in golf than slow play. It's like running your fingernails over a blackboard. It's like a root canal, an IRS audit or a migraine headache.

Eighteen holes of golf should be played in 3 ½ or 4 hours. More than that and I lose interest in my game.

I'm sure there are others like me out there-golfers who prefer a brisk, no-nonsense game. Every year or so, I feel compelled to write a column on slow play."

Elsa Bonstein, writing the "Golf Gab" column for the "Brunswick Beacon," lists 13 suggestions offered by the United States Golf Association (USGA), and then adds her own comments at the end of the article.

I'll capsule my favorite suggestions: Plan your shot before you get to the ball or while others are playing. Line up your putt when others are putting and be ready. Be ready to play when it is your turn. Walk briskly between shots. Walk directly to your ball. Be efficient with pre-shot routine. Take only one practice swing. Play a provisional ball if you think the original might be lost. Exit putting green promptly after holing out. Elsa-"Look ahead, not behind you when you're playing golf. If there is a hole open in front of you, speed up. If you're still lagging behind, ask the group behind you to play through.

When there is a shotgun start and you always finish the round when everyone else is eating dessert, evaluate your play. Perhaps you are a trifle slow.

So there you go, my annual rant on slow play. Move it! Move it! Move it!"

CHAPTER SEVENTEEN

SMOKING?:
STAMP STUPID AND
ADDICTED ON YOUR
FOREHEAD

I AM NOT QUITE sure when my opinion about smoking turned to negative. When I would visit bars or restaurants 15 years ago, there would be no thought given on a choice of "smoking" or "no smoking" sections. With the arrival of allergy problems, I also noticed that the mornings after visits to smoky locations would often bring headaches or a sluggish feeling. Fighting off the allergies, I began to eliminate visits to any location where smoking could affect me. Along with the progress of fighting off the allergies with herbal supplements, I noticed the reduced exposure to smoke was also helpful.

While adjusting to my exposure, I began to notice many of the adverse effects associated with smoking. My research has uncovered a multitude of negative information that I will combine with my personal observations. In order to prepare you for those personal observations, I will begin with my research.

Personally, I hope to scare the shit out of many of you, particularly the smokers. Here is a good start, a study from Erasmus University in the Netherlands of 6,870 men and women 55 years and older, who had no dementia at the beginning of the study. The study found that smokers were twice as likely to develop dementia or Alzheimer's disease. Eighteen million people worldwide are estimated to be afflicted with Alzheimer's, including three percent of those over 60 years old.

One cigarette is enough to impair the function of the heart, making the left ventricle work harder. On a regular basis, this causes increase in the pressure within the ventricle, leading over time to heart trouble or failure. Smoking harms nearly every organ of the body; causing many diseases and reducing the general health of smokers.

It was obvious to me that females were smarter than males in the first 25 years of their lives. This fact certainly shows up in the admission percentages at UNC, now approaching 70% female. The smoking percentages, however, tell a different story. Apparently attempting to lose weight, many females are headed in the opposite direction. According to Cancer Research Campaign, surveying 2,800 11-18 year-old girls, 30% of those who smoked were more likely to be overweight, even though most had started puffing to lose weight. Young girls are "trading pounds" off their weight for years off their life, says Professor Arthur Crisp of the London St. Georges Hospital Medical School. Twenty-five percent of 11-16 year olds in Europe are smokers. The report from England goes a few years back. Updated U.S. information is harsher. First, education is again a large factor. Cigarette smoking estimates are highest for adults with a General Education Development (GED) diploma (46%) or 9-11 years of education (35.4%) and lowest for adults with an undergraduate college degree (9.6%) or a graduate college degree (6.6%).

The adverse health effects from cigarette smoking account for an estimated 438,000 deaths, or nearly one of every five deaths, each year in the United States. More deaths are caused each year by tobacco use than by all deaths from HIV, illegal drug use, alcohol use, motor vehicle injuries, suicides and murders combined. This information is from the Centers for Disease Control and the Journal of the American Medical Association.

Smoking also causes about 90% of lung cancer deaths in women and almost 80% of lung cancer deaths in men. The risk of dying from lung cancer is more than **23** times higher among men who smoke cigarettes, and about **13** times higher among women who smoke cigarettes compared with those who never smoked.

Smoking causes cancers of the bladder, oral cavity, pharynx, larynx (voice box), esophagus, kidney, lung, pancreas, and stomach, and causes acute myeloid leukemia. It also causes coronary heart disease, the leading cause of death in the United States. Cigarette smoking approximately doubles a person's risk for stroke, and reduces circulation by narrowing the blood vessels (arteries).

How about just losing your breath? About 90% of all deaths from chronic obstructive lung disease are attributable to cigarette smoking.

Want to put your baby in danger? Cigarette smoking has many adverse reproductive and early childhood effects, including an increased risk for infertility, preterm delivery, stillbirth, low birth weight, and sudden infant death syndrome (SIDS). **DON'T BE STUPID!!!!!!!!!!!!!!!!!!!!!!!!!!!!**

You've already screwed up your life by smoking. **PLEASE DON'T PASS ON YOUR POISON TO YOUR CHILDREN!!** Give them a damn chance!!

My personal observations are that smokers quite often have ugly teeth, their skin ages prematurely and their hair will also turn gray and disappear at an earlier age. The scent of smoke on clothes and breath permeates in an unpleasant way. I see many smokers who have made bad choices in their personal lives, early pregnancy, choice of abusive partners, and their smoking leads to increased work absences. My last observation may seem to be unusual, and perhaps, insulting. While visiting an old-high school friend in Wilmington about 15 years ago, I was introduced to her friend, an attractive blond that was a ballet instructor. Surprisingly, to me anyway, she was a heavy smoker. Leaving the bar, I was riding to the beach with a good friend of mine. About halfway there, I asked him what he thought of the blond lady. "She was nice and I think she enjoys recreational sex" (I cleaned this one up). The startling statement nearly sobered me up, which was dramatic considering my consumption that night. "Why would you think that?", I asked. Without hesitation, he replied, "she smokes." "Why does that matter?," I inquired. "Women who smoke enjoy recreational sex" (cleansed) was his reply. "Where did you get that from?", I again asked. "I just know..they like having something in their mouth." Laughing hard, I put the "theory" in the back of my mind.

Just a few weeks later, I was again in Wilmington at a waterside restaurant, visiting the same friend. She seemed concerned about something, so I pressed the issue. "I am worried about Jennifer" (the ballet instructor), she said. "Why is that?," I asked. "All she seems interested in is recreational sex." I almost fell backwards out of my chair into the Cape Fear River. The "theory" was confirmed and has been re-confirmed by the actions of other individuals. "Stuff" magazine even released information from a survey that also confirmed the "theory."

I thought the "theory" might give the chapter some balance. Balance or not, think about the smoking. Nothing good can come from it (well, maybe one thing). There are other ways to relax and relieve stress. A number of them are quite fun and even aerobic. Help yourself and please help the kids. Let China and India have the tobacco.

HOW COULD I LEAVE THIS OUT?

The Centers for Disease Control issued a report on the cost of smoking. They determined that each pack of cigarettes sold cost the nation over seven dollars in medical care and productivity. The total was $3,391 for every smoker over a year, a total of **$157.7 BILLION** in lost productivity. The study, conducted from 1995-1999, concluded that the average male smoker loses over **13 years** of his life, while females lose **14 ½ years.** Smoking during pregnancy causes over a thousand infant deaths a year.

Let me make this observation: Allowing employees to take "smoking breaks" is stupid. Why not allow drinking or drug breaks? All are non-productive, and the appearance and smell of a bunch of employees smoking in front of a business is offensive and disgusting.

Many states are facing budget problems. Rising medical costs are a significant culprit in the matter. There is a simple approach, as noted by Dr. Thomas Houston, head of the American Medical Association "Smokeless States Program." "States that raise cigarette taxes not only generate more revenue, but stand to save money in the long run because health care costs associated with smoking diseases will go down as more people quit." Oregon raised its cigarette tax by 60% in 1997, and consumption dropped 20% in the next two years. North Carolina went nearly 15 years without a cigarette tax increase, even during some difficult budget years. Most North Carolina politicians did not have the will to face the tobacco industry. Big tobacco wins-state loses. What did I say earlier about the need to face our problems head on?

Early last summer, I was driving to an appointment in Sarasota, about a 20 mile drive on I-75. About halfway there, traffic comes to virtual halt, and moves only a mile over the next hour. I miss my appointment. Why? Some <u>dumb ass </u>threw his cigarette butt in the median, starting a fire that paralyzed traffic and evacuated a neighborhood. The area is in a drought and this <u>stupid SOB</u> throws his butt into the grassy median. **Addicted and stupid.**

Just as the "dumb ass" endangered the lives of the people, he also littered. I have talked to several people involved with cleanups at beaches and they have all said the dominant dirty item found in large quantities were cigarette butts. Some smart people, non-smokers I am sure, have adopted beach ordinances to prohibit smoking on their beaches, such as Carmel, CA, and Honolulu, HI, among others. Other cities are now approving smoke-free buildings. Good steps, no doubt, but many more are needed.

"Heal," a medical periodical, notes that "Targeting tobacco use has the potential to save perhaps a billion lives in this century." According to Sir Richard Peto of the University of Oxford in England, "Smoking is the main cause of cancer in the world and it is also the main cause of death" among the world's adults. About a billion people smoke and there is a 50% chance it will kill them, says Peto.

Need I say more? If so, you are really are **stupid**…..and **addicted.**

LETTERS FROM AMERICA

"I have noticed that everyone who smokes cigarettes or cigars on the beach disposes of them in the sand on the beach. These people use our beautiful beaches as their own personal ashtray. Smokers throw out their stubs and children and adults have to walk through this waste to get into the water. Have you ever sat next to someone on the beach who is smoking? I have, and I have to say that it burns my eyes and nose. It's a big nuisance."

LINDA BIZZELL

CHAPTER EIGHTEEN

GAYS, REDNECKS & POINT BLANK IDIOTS

THIS CHAPTER <u>WILL</u> insult people of all races, etc., but it is meant to provide both information and direction. A cover of "Newsweek" in August 17, 1998 had a picture of a couple (man & woman) that had recently converted from being gay. A church called the Exodus International, which is a nondenominational Christian fellowship, is dedicated to helping homosexuals change their orientation. In the middle of July, 1998, Exodus, in conjunction with conservative groups, took out full-page ads in major newspapers. The ad offered a bold promise, ex-gays stating "we changed, so can you." Gay advocates were upset, but had no clear evidence of their own that the therapy was not successful. As usual, when you attack one of the "loser" groups, of which homosexuals are often a faction, they cry in despair.

Usually, the cry is for an "ism", such as racism or feminism, but this time it was homophobia. Anne Fausto-Sterling (always worry about the hyphenators) professor of Biology and Woman's Studies at Brown University, called the ads "a deliberate campaign..... to make homophobia acceptable." Well, Ms. Hyphenator, it was acceptable. Most churches do not ordain gays. A "Newsweek" poll at the time revealed that 54% of people interviewed believed that sexual relations between two adults of the same sex is always wrong, according to the General Social Survey of the National Opinion Research Center. Only one-third of the people, and probably most of them from a loser group, believed there is "a lot" of discrimination against gays, and the same percentage approved of legally sanctioned gay marriages. One third of the national poll said homosexuality is something people are born with, but an overwhelming 56% believed that gay men and lesbians can change their sexual orientation through therapy, will power or religious conviction. While Massachusetts (shocker) is allowing gay marriage, the voters of other states spoke otherwise and now 43 states restrict marriage to two persons of the opposite sex. Maine became the first state to reverse a statewide gay rights law prohibiting housing and employment discrimination. The gays have gained grudging acceptance from the other "losers." Due to the mostly liberal media and a party out to buy their votes, they believe they should receive wide acceptance. It should not happen. Personally, I understand lesbianism much more than homosexuality. Somehow, knowing some male wants to "get me from behind," and I can get AIDS from it, has zero appeal for me.

Anyway, where do we start to help these people? One place is with the parents. The story in "Newsweek" relates to a session of the church, where more than half of the 23 men and women acknowledge that they were raped, molested or sexualized as a child. Here we go again with the cycles. Let's examine the additional aspects of homosexuality. Besides the obvious deviant abusive behavior, parents need to monitor their children's self-esteem development and social skills. Sports are an excellent character developer, promoting the social exchange as well as the ability to understand that life has its successes and defeats. Education, again, is vital for knowledge and later career success. The "loser" groups encourage those who struggle with the daily life that it is okay to take the easy way. This has aided in the increase in overweight people and those who abandon the pursuit of the opposite sex as they become physically less attractive. Women, more so than men in my observation, tend to fall into this trap easier. A failed relationship with a male, sometimes the father, also tends to be a stoker for lesbianism. Look around you, particularly in the occupation of landscaping, animal science, law enforcement and to a lesser degree, dental hygiene, and you will see these candidates. Often heavy and usually sporting "butch" type haircuts, these losers gather in their herds and still seem to have continued difficulty with their relationships. I am happy to report that the world's dog population has been spared additional euthanasia as a benefit from the lesbian's preference for the canine species. If you see two women walking down the street with two dogs, I put it in the 90% plus category of a lesbian pair. Similarly, a four-wheel drive vehicle with two women and dog(s) inside is pretty much of a "lock". Playing coed softball, I was directly exposed to many from this group (not from my own team). It appears to me that taking the easy way out has only maintained the lack of happiness in their personal lives.

Let me get a message to these people. Nearly everyone has difficulty with personal relationships. Check the "Relationships" chapter in this book, if you want evidence. It doesn't make you a bad person. Most relationships do not get to marriage and, those that do get there; about half of them end legally. In the lesbian relationships, it appears the lack of success is more than comparable. A little self-motivation can go a long way; get off of your ass and realize that life choices are vital and you are likely heading down the wrong road.

For the guys, watch out for the florists, artists, and some weathermen. If you hear a lisp, perk up your ears and open your eyes. I just hope you don't have to listen to Barney Frank of Massachusetts. If I were from Massachusetts, I wouldn't let anybody know it, unless they want to talk baseball. Kennedy, Frank, Kerry, and a history of bad voting. The limp wrist, of course, is often a giveaway, as well as the use of pink and other bright colors in the wardrobe. I find it difficult to understand that gays are so happy to put their "rainbow" flags on display to publicly state that they are a significant minority that makes a large percentage of the population uncomfortable. But, this is part of the strategy for those making up the "loser group," which, not surprisingly, is similar to the Rainbow Coalition, whose chief spokesperson has been the "Reverend" Jackson. Try to be a squeaky wheel. The gay activists forget that Christians, and other groups have the same right as anyone to shape and influence public opinion. Ads by Christians have been denounced as "extremist." Who are the real extremists?

To point out again the importance of education, there is no need to go any further than to many small towns, where the PBI's (point blank idiots) and rednecks hold fort. While the rednecks would obviously be considered Caucasian, the PBI group also includes blacks, the ever-growing Hispanic problem, and PWT's (poor white trash), who are a huge drain on society. Look for most of the women to be substantially overweight, too many kids (probably beginning with sex in the back of a pickup truck at ages 14-16), many smokers and all doing very little to break this despair cycle for the next generation. The guys drive cars like Firebirds or pickups, often with wrong-sized tires and loud mufflers, have either shag haircuts or more popular now, a crew cut, a preference for tattoos, no shirt or a tank top, a racing bumper sticker or a sticker with a Calvin (of the Calvin & Hobbes cartoon) peeing. Their language is often comparable to that of Gabby Johnson from the movie "Blazing Saddles." It was called "authentic frontier gibberish" in the movie. I call the butchered English "gibby" for short. Speaking of racing; I do somewhat understand the enjoyment of going to a party to see cars moving fast, albeit in an oval or a circle, with the potential of a wreck. Listening to the event on a radio is near torture. It's not difficult to understand why someone would avoid listening to the radio on a Sunday afternoon, when races dominate the airwaves. Between the races and most of the music, I am thankful for CD's and cassettes. Like satellite television, satellite radio is coming to rescue many from the mostly pitiful standard radio programming.

GAY TO STRAIGHT-WHY?

As noted in the story about Exodus International, the cause for a person becoming gay can be the result of the existence of molestation in some form in their life. Anne Heche was molested by her father, dated Ellen DeGeneres for awhile, but has since married Coleman Laffoon and had a son with him. They divorced after five years, and Anne is now with her co-star of "Men In Trees", James Tupper. Anne has stated that she was mentally ill for 31 years after the molestation of her father, a minister.

DOG THEORY

Martina Navratilova-"I can't imagine my life without a dog. A house without a dog is empty. We are fostering dogs." The great tennis star has at least 12 in her house.

CHAPTER NINETEEN

THE ROLLER COASTER RIDE OF RELATIONSHIPS

I HAVE ALWAYS BEEN active in the pursuit of the opposite sex, beginning at the Little Red Schoolhouse in kindergarten. There, I would chase down girls for a kiss during our time on the playground. During elementary school, I had a "girlfriend" from grades first through fourth, with an ego-deflating breakup during the summer after fourth grade. This was the first of several negative relationship closures that would dig into my self-confidence over the next 25 years. The next "bad ending" was after seventh grade, then after ninth, and the worst following my freshman year in college after a three-year relationship. While both of us were undergoing changes and I stumbled through my freshman year with mediocre (?) grades as well as two traffic accidents in ten days, the ending was a majority of my fault. I was significantly self-centered (and want to stop talking about myself soon) and this ego shot and realization was to be a large factor in my life for nearly seven years. My last three years of college, one year of graduate school at Ohio State (hell for the four months of winter) and first two years at Oklahoma were mostly a compilation of infrequent one-night stands, heavier drinking and some "funny smoke" during the college days. There was also some lonely soul-searching and the beginning of learning more about myself. I began to develop a stronger streak of independence.

During my last year at Oklahoma as Athletic Ticket Manager, I got a close up look at the greed and self-centeredness of Coach Barry Switzer. More importantly, I began the first steps toward my first marriage. The ticket and business offices worked close together and I had my eye caught by a young (18) lady. She reminded me of the late Princess Diana. While attending a post-game celebration in Miami in January of 1980, we locked stares and decided to dance (under obviously heavy alcohol influence). A little while later, I laid a near attack kiss on her in an elevator of the International Hotel. It was as if seven years of energy was consumed in one passionate kiss. After returning to Norman from the bowl, we were nearly inseparable for the next six months. I had never experienced a hormone push every day at work, but fortunately there was satisfaction in the PM, where we spent nights at my rented home or in her dormitory.

In early December of 1979, I had the chance to interview for a position back in Chapel Hill at the Rams Club. My father had been a volunteer for the Rams Club since 1959, overseeing the investments and accounting. He provided significant administrative assistance to a staff that was too small, lacking in administrative skills, and resistant to change. Surprisingly, the existing Assistant Athletic Director was chosen for the position. Little was I to know that this choice was pre-determined and the person hired would interview me for the same job just seven months later after he became Athletic Director. At the time, I had respect for this person, but in less than three years, he would become the centerpiece of my deep disgust for the ultimate symbol of greed, self-importance, and absence of ethics.

So, in July of 1980, I was offered the position of Assistant Executive Vice-President of The Rams Club, receiving a salary increase from 16 to 21K and the opportunity to come home. I could not turn it down, that decision was easy enough. There was a tougher decision staring right at me. What should I do about the now six-month old relationship? Certainly, it was on the right track for a potential long-term success, but what would be the correct decision now? Could I leave her and hope that somehow a long-distance relationship might be maintained? Was it fair to ask a 19 year-old single-child female to leave home unmarried, and move 1,200 miles in the hope that our relationship would prosper? The answer was marriage, which we did on August 20, 1980 in a small town near Muskogee, OK. Several of my closer friends and family were there for the ceremony in an amphitheater on a lake. It was a beautiful setting and the song list included Paul McCartney's "Nineteen Hundred and Eighty-Five" from the "Band on the Run" album. Great song, Paul, please play it on your next tour as the pianist butchered it that day. Perhaps, that was a sign of things to come; I had written my own vows, consisting of four lines stolen from two songs, but froze after issuing the first line. Somehow, the ceremony was completed.

Have you heard of the stress meter? I wish I had known about it in 1980. Moving, marriage, and a new job are all near the top of the list. I've always liked a challenge, but this must have been too much at once. I had already started work prior to the marriage, so, after the wedding weekend, I returned to work. My bride came to Chapel Hill two weeks later and we had a short honeymoon on the N.C. coast. Due to the near beginning of classes at Carolina, it was difficult to find a place to live in Chapel Hill, even with all of my parent's contacts (they had lived in Chapel Hill since 1951). Finally, we secured a 400 square-foot apartment on the ground floor, near an entrance, in a complex near downtown. I often walked to work; looking back, the beginning of that walk was along the same path where an UNC law student later had a shooting spree that killed two and permanently damaged the hand of a Chapel Hill police officer. The murderer was found innocent due to insanity and was initially awarded $500,000 in a case against his psychiatrist. I'll address that in another book.

My wife began searching for a job and secured a secretarial position with the University. She seemed reasonably happy with it, but the cramped apartment and my stern job focus was starting to put us on edge. We chose to look for a rental house and finally located a nice sized house in a desirable neighborhood. It was winter now and there was a reason, unknown to us, that the house was available. The house was heated by oil, which was used up quickly. The poorly insulated house ran up a $400 oil bill in January, 1981, and we were distraught. After some haggling with the rental agent, she let us out of the six-month lease. Fortunately, a couple I had gotten to know through my work in the UNC Ticket Office had a condominium available and we moved there, but only for a month. A local real estate agent and friend of my parents offered to finance a mortgage and half of a down payment on a new house in Carrboro, the sister town of Chapel Hill. Hopefully, this was to be somewhat of a "new beginning," allowing us to refocus on our relationship. Unfortunately, too many negatives had developed as my wife fought homesickness, feeling alone without friends and realizing that I had not been able to find a balance between work and marriage. There was a comfort level of support for me with good friends and family close by; she did not have that support. In June, she left for a week for a "vacation" that was really a trial separation. By Halloween, the strain reached a peak and the marriage was over. Oddly, the decision to end the marriage seemed to relax much of the pressure, and we began to enjoy each other. She flew home the day before Thanksgiving. Upon returning from the airport, my emotions seemed to all erupt at once. With my focus on the job, I had been in denial about my feelings. The denial was a definite setback personally and would affect me negatively in my next few relationships. Any personal relationship progress that I had made seemed lost. The strain of the deteriorating relationship, too many moves and continued internal job pressure had taken its toll. The result was a feeling of guilt and a drop in confidence. My wife and I did stay in touch by phone, which played a significant part in my life over the next year. Without the day-to-day pressures that had previously existed for us, we maintained a comfortable relationship. She had gone back to school in Oklahoma and was doing well with it. Obviously, the distance between us reduced any opportunity for the relationship to begin anew, but enough was there for the contact to continue on a somewhat regular basis. Was this good? How many long-distance serious relationships do you know about that have worked? I believe it is nearly impossible to effectively build a lasting relationship without regular personal contact and communication.

Things would soon change on my personal side. Our office was in the middle of a nearly four year campaign to raise money for the, then, largest athletic-fund raising campaign ever. The campaign would build the Dean E. Smith Student Activities Center. A professional fund-raising group had been hired to lead the campaign, which was a definite mistake. Fund-raising for athletics should be left to those involved in it. The campaign was dragging, but the second place NCAA finish in 1981 and national championship in 1982 helped spur the campaign to surging success. Seven million dollars in pledges were made during the last six weeks of the campaign in 1984. Anyway, thanks to Coach Smith, Michael Jordan, James Worthy, Sam Perkins, Jimmy Black, Al Wood, Roy Williams, Bill Guthridge, and many others.

Anyway, again feeling alone in the lousy month of February, I was happy to hear from one of my co-workers, who I will talk about later, that one of the student helpers had been complimentary of my looks. In a weakened state, I responded with a call and the relationship began to progress. Let me again restate my weakened condition. By 1982, we were into year two of the fund-raising campaign. The fund-raising was in addition to our regular jobs. As noted, my job was a tremendous challenge, as approximately a third of our contributors were at <u>least</u> 12 months behind with their annual dues requirements. One "group" of members had been receiving benefits to which they were not entitled. I was to become the enforcer, including heading the implementation of a new priority system, a change fought by my superior in numerous ways. Another of my responsibilities had been involvement in the travel plans for large Rams Club groups to special events, such as the Final Four or to Hawaii for an early basketball season tournament. In February, I flew with a travel agent to Hawaii to inspect hotels for the Rams Club trip to Honolulu for the Rainbow Classic. We arrived late in the afternoon and I was exhausted, not helped by the consumption of four beers (now I know why alcohol is not recommended while flying). Our job began early the next day and by day's end, we had previewed seven hotels, choosing the Illikai, the location where many scenes from "Hawaii 5-0" were filmed. We miss you, Steve. It's hard to beat when McGarrett (Steve) would get pissed on the show and who could ever forget the famous "Book 'Em Danno!" Anyway, our business done, we decided to leave on Saturday, less than 48 hours after arriving in Honolulu. Back at work on Monday, I had discovered double jet lag. In late March, the Final Four plans were a nightmare. New Orleans was a racket, no thanks to some tour operator named Abbott. Hotel rooms that were contracted one day were gone the next morning. Along with assisting in the ticket preparation, I was only able to get seven hours of sleep in four days, including 43 straight hours with no sleep. Once in New Orleans, a few more hours of sleep, adrenaline, and the national championship kept me going. Offering to be flexible due to the scarcity of rooms, I was registered at four different hotels in four days, including two in one day. On the morning of the day of the two semi-final games, I registered at the Holiday Inn Superdome. Returning to the hotel after the games, I was informed that I no longer had a room. It was worth it to win the first national championship in 25 years on the night Michael Jordan started his collection of game-winning shots, swishing the jumper with 17 seconds left to give Carolina a 63-62 win. Upon returning to Chapel Hill, there was another project for me, one that I had only minimal preparation time for prior to the Final Four.

My second summer job in high school was working at the University golf course, providing maintenance assistance. Since I was on the high school golf team, this was enjoyable for me. My second boss at the golf course later became UNC golf coach and he and I remained friends. He knew of my interest in golf and asked if I would be tournament director for the 1982 Division I Golf Championships, since Carolina was the host school. The tournament was to be played at the famous Pinehurst No. 2 course. I was asked by a friend; it seemed like a challenge and a privilege, so I accepted the job. Several trips to Pinehurst prior to the tournament were required for preparations. Organizing a large golf tournament correctly is a difficult job. Thanks to the local volunteers, the "Tin Whistles," Pinehurst golf staff, friends from the business of athletics, the Carolina Sports Information Staff, and the cooperation of many coaches, we pulled off a very commendable job. How many hours? Seven straight seven to elevens, or a 112-hour week. On the drive home after the tournament, in a preview of future problems, I apparently fell asleep at the wheel, albeit briefly. I drove through a stop sign and down a hill toward a cemetery before coming back to life. It was a warning that was missed. I'll try to get back on track, but the stress meter was again on high. Certainly, I would advise everyone to strive to keep the meter down as often as possible. It can sharply affect your decision-making, but even more important are the health negatives.

The new relationship developed into a long-distance one as she moved back home after completing her senior year. Her parents, nice people who I continued contact with over the years, welcomed me to their home and beach house in the summer. Trips were made back and forth as the relationship grew more serious. As we moved to the fall, Carolina's football team was ranked as high as number two in the preseason and headed to Three Rivers Stadium to play Pitt, the No. 1 team in some of the polls. Dan Marino was the Pitt quarterback, but Carolina did a terrific job against him, intercepting four passes. Unfortunately, the Carolina offense could only make two field goals and the game was lost, 7-6. It continued the trend of Carolina football being unable to win the "big" game, a pattern that has continued until today. Perhaps, finally, Coach Butch Davis is the one to stop the pattern.

I noticed a feeling of sluggishness in September, which continued throughout the month. A daily jogger at the time, I was sure a little more sleep and regular exercise would get me back to normal. On a warm late summer day, I took off on my regular course through the UNC campus. After the seventh stop on a 3 ½ mile run, and difficulty breathing, I knew there was trouble beyond feeling tired. That night, under the care of my latest, my temperature ballooned to 104. It certainly ranked among the worst I had ever felt. As a good friend of mine would agree, having bronchitis is somewhat akin to one foot in the grave. Fortunately, the antibiotics worked quickly.

The football season was a great disappointment. After back-to-back top ten poll finishes, the Heels finished 7-4 in the regular season and were selected to play Texas in the Sun Bowl. Ticket sales were near nothing and instead of going to Hawaii for the basketball tournament, where I had helped make the travel arrangements, I was asked by the athletic director to go to El Paso for the week. Glad to be going to the bowl, but disappointed to miss the trip to Hawaii, I was hoping El Paso would earn its reputation as the "Sun City." It started well at 70 degrees when we arrived, but would get worse every day as we headed to the Christmas Day game, where it ended up snowing. Strangely, this week also included a slight career change. The athletic director had discussed the idea of my taking over the ticket office for the retiring ticket manager, who provided much of my training in tickets when I worked in the ticket office during college. She was a personal friend, and married to a delightful man named "Sarge," who was the equipment manager and jack-of-all-trades for the athletic department. While it appeared she was being shoved out the door, I did not blame her for wanting to leave the ticket business.

In El Paso, the athletic director and I met one night in the hotel bar to discuss the new job. He was offering a nice salary increase, but I wanted more money and a higher title. I settled for his money without the title, believing I would be rewarded if the job was done successfully. Carolina was seriously entering the computer age, as The Rams Club was purchasing complete hardware and software to go on line in late 1982. The previously mentioned co-worker and I were the main developers of the software in cooperation with a local computer company headed by Dave Dickson, a dedicated, generous Carolina fan. It was a difficult challenge, but I feel she and I did a very credible job. Needing more room for the computer equipment (large in those days), she and I moved to the "dungeon," an area underneath the stands in Carmichael Auditorium, which was the building for Carolina basketball. No windows, but plenty of paper-loving cockroaches. The air-conditioning unit was inside the area and leaked frequently. It was a definite unhealthy office; one that took a toll on both of us.

The plan was for me to move into the Ticket Office in April, the time we started working on the upcoming football season. Ticket demand was strong after the bowl game win and a new policy focused on limiting the number of preferred tickets a contributor could reorder. This made our already large job much bigger. I was fortunate to inherit an experienced staff. In particular, the present assistant had become both a friend and effective co-worker. Her dedication over the next nine months was a major reason we were able to accomplish our difficult job. First, there was the major reassignment of seats as a result of the new policy. The process of informing the contributors of the change was a difficult one, but we communicated the necessary information without much negative reaction. The change also increased contributions by over $300,000 in the first year and over $500,000 in the second year.

Our job was big, and made larger by heavy ticket demand. The hours were long, but would grow outrageously later in the year. We were happy to finish the process of assigning the season tickets by early August. I parked my dealer-provided Oldsmobile Delta 88 outside the Ticket Office and we loaded numerous trays of tickets until the car was completely packed. In celebration, we rang a cowbell down the street on the way to the Post Office.

Back to stress, as my own escalated in 1983. My relationship had its moments, but there were warning signals. Past relationships, erratic behavior, and a growing urgency from her to get married should have been enough for me to step back from marriage. My first failure created a desire to want to do it right, which can be a personality flaw. In a weakened state, I was headed toward a mistake. It is essential to learn about yourself to avoid making poor relationship decisions. If you do this correctly, your instincts will be stronger and you will be more likely to make good decisions.

In the summer, I was out jogging in Wrightsville Beach, NC, and literally collapsed from heat exhaustion. Work would get busier as the football team started 7-0 and rose to number three in the polls. Expectations were sky-high in basketball with Michael back and the team blew away its opposition on the way to winning its first 21 games. Unfortunately, an extreme cheap shot foul by LSU's John Tudor on a breakaway layup by Kenny Smith caused Smith to break his wrist in the 18th game and the starting point guard would not be the same upon his return later in the season.

As we began work for the basketball season, the workload rose to an insane level. Jane, the assistant, and I worked a six-week period of 8 AM to 2 AM workdays in October and November, including some weekends. It culminated in a 24-hour marathon on a late Saturday in November. Carolina was at home against Duke in the first night game at Kenan Stadium, but Jane and I had so much work to do that we could not even go to the game. The football team had collapsed after losing at Maryland, 28-26 in the eighth game, losing three straight before finding a way to barely beat Duke that night. The win gave Carolina a bid to the Peach Bowl , where we had normally sold a significant number of tickets. Faced with additional work on top of our already overloaded schedule of the last six weeks, I found myself in the halls of Carmichael Auditorium loudly cursing the prospects of a bowl game at six AM on Sunday morning.

Fortunately, there was light at the end of the tunnel. The athletic director, perhaps sensing that I would be reluctant to cooperate with his "ticket deals," offered me the opportunity to go back to full-time duties in the Rams Club, which I was happy to accept, again. We hired the ticket manager of the Triple A baseball Louisville Cardinals to replace me in early December. A quiet, soft-spoken person when he arrived, the job drove him to become a fiery and free-speaking ticket manager by the time he left in 1992. This is the nature of the ticket business. Many of the people calling are only worrying about their personal situation, and you have to develop a rigid side to handle the tough calls. It is my theory that this leads most people in the ticket business to have a loose tongue. The new ticket manager and I would often argue loudly in the office on purpose, usually about the same subject, which was a stress release for us and perhaps provided some comic relief to others in the ticket office. It was like Oklahoma all over again, but with less people and less stress relief. Tickets are a stressful business, particularly at a school where the demand has remained high for so many years. It's a big business, evidenced by the fact that a $100,000 contribution will only get you the right to buy two basketball seats, most likely in the upper level. We also sold 1,200 new box seats for football in six months with a minimum contribution of $30,000 for two seats. At the start of that box seat campaign in 1995, we were in the latter stages of a disappointing football season.

As December moved rapidly, the "marriage" pressure arose to become an ultimatum. Through most of my decisions, I rely on my gut feeling for the answers, a trait I believe that was mostly passed on by my father. This one did not feel right, but a combination of my guilt from the first marriage and a stressed out mental state led me to agree to a wedding on April 7, 1984. I was 30 years old, she was 23. She was too young, among a few other things, and I ignored my own warnings. Things were not all bad, but problems arose in short order. Three weeks before the wedding, another of her secrets was uncovered, on an issue we had previously discussed. I came dangerously close to calling off the wedding, as most of my friends had advised me to do anyway. I worried about the embarrassment to her parents, a delightful couple that I called Mom and "Doc" for quite awhile, and my own parents. My three siblings were, and still are, married with children and I thought it would also bother them.

I should have read my own warning signs, such as attempting to drink a beer per hole the day before the wedding. Playing with my brother and close friends, I was only one beer short. Retiring to her parent's beach house about 20 minutes away, the beer kept all of us asleep too long and I was late for the rehearsal. She was rightfully very upset, but it did not seem to matter that much to me. In fact, the drinking restarted at the rehearsal dinner. I paid for my indulgence, feeling hung over and looking a bit pale for the ceremony in the chapel, not the church, the next day. The highlight of the ceremony was the playing and singing of the McCartney song, "Warm and Beautiful." Too bad I did not share the sentiment of the song.

After a week in Hilton Head that was quite relaxing, we settled into the house in Carrboro. She found a job as a teacher's aide. I began to experience numerous, energy-shattering headaches in the later summer and early fall. At first, I thought that my only problem was being a bit tired. Finally, I made a visit to a local ENT doctor, Paul Biggers, whose personality was a delightful mixture of kindness, concern and humor. Add that to his expert skills as a doctor and you can see that I was in good hands. Paul worked to find my problem and was able to provide temporary relief in the first couple of visits. Finally, one day, he inserted a long wire into my nose that had a cotton tip with a dab of medication on it. Instantly, for the first time in months, I had complete relief. I requested more of the medication, only to be told that cocaine was an ingredient in the medication. Paul's plan was to shrink the spur deep in my head with a medication. The plan had moderate success, but time seemed to reduce the effectiveness of the medication. The only alternative for a permanent solution was surgery, basically to chisel out the spur. Surgery was in February of '85, early one morning. I only had a local, which meant that I got to sense the chisel effect. It could have been unnerving, but Dr. Biggers kept me loose with his delightful bedside manner and humor.

The first 48 hours of recovery seemed to be okay and the headaches were gone. However, a different pain arrived that grew constantly. A night's sleep was lost until a visit to the doctor determined that the stitches were exhibiting little flexibility, creating a pinching effect. The stitches were cut and there was relief. The only other significant pain occurred when the packing in my nose was removed. Hoping to put this problem behind me, I went back to work after missing only seven days. This may have been a mistake without the stitch issue, but the lack of recovery time would cost me dearly. As Kyle says in many "South Park" episodes, I learned something, but not quickly enough. Already stressed out from the last four years and not allowing sufficient recovery time from the surgery, my body would begin to show signs of weakness. Later that summer, after bouts with congestion and some shortness of breath, it was determined that I had pleurisy. There was constant mucus and an overall lack of energy, which was contrary to my usual pace. The problem would linger, and, along with the work and personal stress, would eventually weaken my immune system to the point of developing allergies.

My problems with the athletic director continued and reached a peak in December of 1984. The Rams Club raised the funds to build the new basketball arena based on a diagrammed number and location of seats. Being the most successful athletic fund-raising project to date, we were proud of the success, having made every effort to "do it right," and allocate the seating as promised. Earlier in the fall, there had been evidence of a student revolt against the location of UNC student seating. Even though the students chose not to contribute any funds toward the project, it was their position (or the opinion of a few "leaders") that they were entitled to more and better lower level seats. Never mind that the total student allocation would almost double; this was lost in the argument. Pressured by the students, the athletic director pressed hard for the commitment to help the students. Part of his strategy was to provide only the facts that would support his case. Reminded me of Bill Clinton. I, however, feeling that the policy-making committee was depending on my ticket experience, presented the whole story and the commitment was rejected. My initial reaction was simply that the committee had made the proper decision. After the meeting, one of those present said that the athletic director had appeared upset, but this was not confirmed to me until about three weeks later. The athletic director called me into his office to say that he had been unable to talk with me until that time due to his anger. He thought I had been disloyal and my response was that all of the facts should be presented. Leaving the office, I felt bewildered and resentful. This was not supposed to happen at Carolina, and the combination of the spur and the brewing battle with the athletic director was taking its toll. The fund-raising campaign for the basketball arena reached closure in August. It was difficult to even answer all of the phone calls during the last six weeks of the campaign. I wondered at times if the pressure and stress would ever subside, but at the same time the challenge and pleasure of doing it at Carolina was mostly fulfilling.

Unfortunately, the seating issue came to a head late in the year. Prior to the meeting on the issue, the athletic director called in three of our staff members to suggest that we not say anything that "might embarrass the University." After my earlier meeting with the Athletic Director, I knew what the suggestion was meant to do. We met in December at the N.C. High School Athletic Association and I attended with facts in hand. Only certain committee members were supposed to be present, but the athletic director invited several guests who were apparent "plants" (Hillary tactic) to support his agenda. One of these "plants" spoke at length of the necessity to provide the tickets to the students.

In addition to screwing the Rams Club, the athletic director also sold out the faculty and staff at Carolina. After much discussion, the Rams Club relinquished the seats in question, but received a comparable number of seats in another location that was taken from the proposed faculty and staff allotment. This was not the correct answer to me. We had raised the funds based on specific seats being available (the athletic director had done little to aid the fund-raising) and now the rules were being changed. The old "bait and switch." During the meeting, I was asked several times about the overall ticket situation and whether the seats in question should be given to the students. Struggling to be honest without "embarrassing the University," I provided as much information as possible without expressing my opinion. I could feel the blood rushing to my face as the frustration mounted inside of me. Our President at the time, trying to make a proper decision, pleaded for the staff to provide opinions, even to the point of saying "I believe the staff is reluctant to respond."

Seeing my value system and principles and beliefs in Carolina under heavy attack, I exploded out of the meeting. My wife tried to console me, but this incident pushed me over the edge. After a drive and a few tears of anger, I quickly consumed several beers. This was both a hard lesson and a wakeup call. I must have been naïve, but the damage would linger. The stress meter soared again and it would be over two years before the anger would begin subsiding. A rage and deep cynicism developed from the incident that significantly affected my personality. The pleurisy and beginnings of the decline of the marriage served only to exaggerate the problem. My wife had decided she wanted to go back to school, another detail not discussed prior to marriage. Feeling isolated and hypersensitive to anyone exhibiting self-centeredness, I began to build upon my negative feelings. A new conflict also arose; we were living in the same house that I shared with my first wife. This one continues to baffle me, even though I faced it twice in three years. Why did it matter? Memories? Why not sell the bed? How many other memories were significant? Anyway, this "problem" persisted for over a year until one Sunday morning when I actually got up early and checked the real estate section. A house was for sale in a neighborhood that was adjacent to the one where I grew up. Tucked away, but close to town and the campus, it was an older house with almost twice as much room as the present house. Sure, there was work to be done on updating the house, but it was a classic case of location, location, location. My wife was somewhat appeased and we made an offer that day at full price. Considering there were seven other full-price offers within a week, we were fortunate. The owner was a widowed man, whose age had crept on him and he was happy to sell the house to someone he knew. His daughter was a friend of my younger sister. Tragically, the mother had died after falling out of a window while painting the house.

My marriage had not been going particularly well. I had some hope that the change might improve the relationship. After all of the talk about a different house, she appeared uninterested in aiding the effort of sweat equity. Wallpaper had to be removed, among many other things, and she was not there. With all of the complaining about the other house, it was a severe blow to the relationship and it was quickly downhill from there. Summer moved to fall and her threats of leaving began in earnest. At that point, I had little desire or energy to pour into our relationship. Work had become a drag, and for the first time since my return to Chapel Hill, I seriously considered leaving Carolina. One of our contributors, who had become a close friend, had begun looking at purchasing the rights to TCBY in various cities. One of those cities was Syracuse, NY, which I considered one of the ugliest cities in the United States. Still, at the time, it seemed to be worthwhile to examine the situation there. It was a weekend in late September and we planned a whirlwind trip to cover the area. I was still working hard at my job and was not feeling much better physically. Whether or not this was the cause, or perhaps it was done subconsciously, but I completely forgot that the weekend included my wife's birthday. Upon my return, she informed me what I had done, or not done, and that she had indulged herself with a shopping spree for clothes. While not proud of my omission, it was an obvious sign of the state of the relationship. Soon after, she informed me of a definite date for her departure, which was December 5th. I personally was quite relieved and our relationship seemed to improve the next two months. Meanwhile, my friend and I continued to pursue TCBY, but moved our focus to Charleston, SC. Preferring warm weather, I was happier to be looking there and my potential partner had previously lived there. We moved forward and reached a tentative agreement to buy the four existing stores in the Charleston area and add four more in the next two years. Based on our observations, two of the existing stores were in productive locations, one was fair, and the last was poor. Still, we moved forward and I was enrolled for a school at TCBY headquarters. My family was terribly upset, particularly my father, who had been the most proud of my return to Chapel Hill. He wrote me an impassioned four page letter exhorting me to stay in my job. A few days later, my younger sister called, crying on the phone, pleading with me to stay, voicing concern over our father's reaction, including his health. I thought the call was unfair to me, but appreciated my sister's concern.

Not wanting to cause any problems for the Rams Club, I informed my boss and the athletic director that, pending completion of our business deal, my resignation would be effective the following week. The athletic director, perhaps happy to see my departure, quickly informed the department of the news. My future partner had his accountant produce additional financial projections and he called just two days before my scheduled departure. The deal was called off; he indicated the additional projections had revealed income deficiencies. My response was a serious mix of feelings. First, there was the relief for a decision. Second, the excitement of a new deal was gone, Third, I had the sense that fate had lent a hand. My friend gave me few details in the 90 minute conversation, but he had many years of successful experience with Burger King, so I had the sense not to question his knowledge. Considering the state of the yogurt business just a few years later, he made the correct decision. To this day, I have not asked him whether there were other factors involved in his decision. Despite the awkward retractions at work, I came back to the Rams Club with a renewed sense of purpose, and living alone again added to the freshness. The freshness was helped by the hiring of a new boss, someone I had supported strongly for the job. The athletic director had his designs on putting a spy or puppet in the position, but I worked behind the scenes with members of the Executive Committee to prevent his attempt. Nice try, but the devious one would lose this battle.

Only a few days after my wife had moved out on a weekend in December, I had a visit at my office from my ex-employee. By bizarre coincidence, she lived in the same apartment complex where my wife had moved to and the complex newsletter listed new occupants. She and I had generally worked well together, the software development being one example. She had unexpectedly resigned about two months after my marriage. I was about to find out the reason.

My father had resigned from his job as Senior Vice-President at NCNB (now Bank of America) after 37 years with the same bank. It had begun as the Bank of Chapel Hill. He was a hard worker, known for his dedication, firmness and fairness. By the end of his career, he had tired of the banking business, as it became more de-personalized. The retirement party was set for early April and

I hoped that the focus would be on the retirement, not the fact that my wife was not there. She and I had maintained infrequent communication and I thought it was appropriate to ask her to attend the function. She had enjoyed a good relationship with my father. We talked a few times about it, but on a Friday night, just days before the party, she rejected the invitation. Furious, I called my ex-employee, who had offered to "talk" if I had the need. She was receptive, and armed with a 12 pack of beer, I went to her apartment. We talked, watched movies, and cuddled late into the night. That night and morning began the relationship. All went well at first, but slowly our differing approaches to life created problems. Even though I felt I was still being the same person, she began to find problems with my choice of music, McCartney in particular. This was strange since she was a Beatle fan. My driving, patiently aggressive, was another problem and so was, generally, my overall personality. We broke up several times and I worked hard to put things back together. The ex-wife living in the house problem arose again, so I agreed, quite reluctantly to start looking at other houses. We found one south of town that was bigger, more modern, and had a pool. The initial asking price for the house was $172,000, but it had been chopped to $159,000. Just to show my interest to my future live-in, I offered $140,000. They quickly countered with $152,000. Deciding to get the process over quickly, I offered a final price of $145,000. The house had been donated to the Habitat for Humanity, and their representatives were ready to sell at 145. Despite our troubles, we decided to move in together. Again, initially things went well. She had a teenage daughter and our relationship seemed quite comfortable. But, old difficulties arose again. The combination of her definite areas of dislike for me, and my stubbornness created growing pressure. In early December, I went to Chicago to see McCartney at the Rosemont Horizon. I had seen him once before, in 1976. Oddly enough, I met my live-in's sister in Chicago for the concert. She and I had been friends through the athletic department and shared a deep admiration of Paul. After John Lennon was shot in 1980, we were worried that Paul might not tour again. We were not disappointed, yelling loudly after nearly every song, and both of us shed tears of joy. The second night was musically equal, but we had a loud Mexican behind us who thought it was funny to show both his ass and his inability to sing.

Returning home, I had no inquiries about my trip. She seemed to have no interest in the fact that I had enjoyed myself, or in any other aspect of the trip.

The negativity of the relationship had begun to wear on me, so one night while talking in bed, I blurted out that things were not working and she should move out. This was one of my "gut" decisions that I have become more reliant on as time has passed. The next three weeks were uncomfortable as I moved across the hall, and we shared an uneasy Christmas. Moving day for her was the day after Christmas, and I decided to head to my beach house. The decision to purchase the house, with a close friend as partner, had been one of my best from a personal and financial standpoint. Unfortunately, a deep freeze had frozen the pipes in the house and I had to stay with a realtor (thanks, Ann) for the night. My buddy, plumber Dave Deavor, who later called me a "tick turd," came and fixed the pipes. Considering the stress of the breakup and the normal busy holiday season, the beach stay was excellent tonic.

Returning on December 31st, I had a call from my just departed roommate. She invited me over to her apartment and we brought in the New Year in the same manner that we started our relationship 30 months earlier, this time with champagne rather than beer. It appeared that reconciliation was possible, and we agreed to go to counseling to work out our differences. I thoroughly enjoyed the opportunity to discuss my relationship and approach to life with an objective listener. We never made it to a joint session, which I think would have been very useful.

Later in the winter, her father's health began to fail due to cancer. He was an enjoyable person, and we shared a love of most sports. He had been a highly successful high school football coach. For a brief time, he lived in a retirement community, but his failing health had forced his three daughters to choose a rest home. As things got worse, I used to visit him every day at lunch during the week, often taking him a piece of pie that he enjoyed after a routine meal. After a few months, he was doing poorly. I had to go to Myrtle Beach for a local Rams Club organizational meeting, which was held over lunch. While at the restaurant, I received a call from my ex that he had died. The crowd was at the restaurant, so the meeting was held, as was one in Wilmington that evening. After the Wilmington function, I called her and she cried deeply. I rushed home the next day, and accompanied her to the funeral and burial. It seemed that her sharing of grief may have reopened the possibility of a reunion, but nothing further developed. Through all of the time spent in this relationship, I felt a significant sense of progress. First, if you have to work too hard on a relationship, it is unlikely to last. The energy spent on keeping things together will eventually become a burden and much enjoyment will be bypassed. Second, it is most helpful to be close friends, as it provides protection from the low times. Third, do not be too proud or afraid of losing your own judgment if you believe you need an objective outside opinion. While I did not use the counseling very long (thanks, Ken), it both reassured me and opened my eyes in regards to relationships.

I felt content and confident after the end of the relationship. Not too long after, I went out with two ladies terrified of getting involved and a few other situations that will be kept silent for now. In late 1993, the wife of one of my men's softball teammates arranged a semi-blind date for me. The wife, a female friend and the date and I attended the Vince Gill-Mary Chapin Carpenter concert at the Smith Center. We listened to Mary Chapin and loved it, then watched part of the Vince Gill performance. He's a talented guitarist, but I liked her style of music better. After leaving, the wife and friend decided to go home early, conveniently allowing just the two of us to spend some together. She had very recently been through a difficult breakup with cheating involved and was also about halfway through her first year of graduate business school at Carolina. I believe she was half-duped into this semi-blind date, but we had a nice visit at a downtown restaurant afterwards and began to see each other infrequently. There was no doubt that I was the aggressor who kept the contact going for the next couple of months. Meanwhile, a couple from Charlotte had called me about dating his sister-in-law. The funny thing about this was I had a previous relationship with his wife during college. Trying to be open and honest after my new friend had endured the cheating of her last relationship, I told her about my offer. The reaction was strange, "I don't think I'd like that" and then, "I think you should leave." A bit confused, I left to ponder the situation. Deciding to decline the date offer, I pursued a beach trip on the first weekend of March with my friend and her daughter to my cottage. We left after work on a Friday and arrived after 9 PM. One problem; my house was rented for the weekend. Not even thinking a renter would be there on the first weekend of March, I had not checked with the rental agency. Fortunately, I had developed some friends during my four years of ownership. My realtor in the purchase, a delightful woman named Connie, came to my rescue. Knowing that I was bringing my friend, Connie had sent flowers to the cottage. The people staying in my house had thought it was a nice greeting from the rental agency, but Connie informed me otherwise. The renters let me pursue a solution by phone and Connie arranged for us to stay in a duplex owned and inhabited on one side by one of her fellow realtors, Gay Atkins. It was two bedrooms, on the ocean, and certainly sufficient for our stay. The flowers helped too.

Despite the time of year, we enjoyed the day on Saturday, walking the beach and watching television. We decided on takeout for dinner and then settled down to watch Carolina play Duke in Durham. Spurred on by the Heels' play and wine, we enjoyed a delightful evening. The daughter crashed early, leaving the two of us cuddled on the couch. Just like six years previously, minus the horror movies, the relationship reached a new level. Leaving the beach, I believed that this might be the one.

All went well, and school got easier. We went to the beach often, even to my own house a few times. She would sleep in the third bedroom, but I would usually "tuck her in" at night. The daughter, and sometimes a friend, would stay in the second bedroom. As it got closer to her graduation from business school, we discussed the possibility of them moving in with me. Unlike my first live-in attempt, this relationship seemed to be thriving. I had the daughter's bedroom fixed to order and they moved in soon after the graduation. All seemed to be going well for awhile. The daughter was gone much of the summer to camp, and the two of us enjoyed our time together. She was training in Boston for a few weeks and we had a great weekend trip to Perkins Cove in Maine. We also visited Nantucket over the July 4th weekend. Once school started in the fall, the whole situation started to unravel. One of the daughter's friends, in particular, was a difficulty for me. She was loud, desperate, not particularly bright, and basically exhibited all the negative qualities of a Yankee. More on that later. My companion and I disagreed on the idea of keeping certain people away from her daughter. A sense of isolation and being taken for granted began to engulf me. For the most part, I stayed out of any disciplinary matters until an incident with alcohol occurred at my house one afternoon after school. The daughter's friend mentioned earlier was involved. The difference of approach in discussing the matter with the daughter was a major negative and seemed to accelerate the decline of the relationship. Under the stress of the deteriorating home situation and busy and difficult basketball season, my health showed signs of suffering. The big H problem in my backside occurred twice within the period of a few months, prompting a visit to the doctor after frequent bleeding. Carolina went to the Final Four in Indianapolis and the week of the event was flat out hectic. It is always a dream to go to a Final Four, but few people realize how difficult it is for the people handling the tickets. Allocations have to be decided upon, demand has to be accurately determined, and names attached to tickets. For the first time, it seemed the ticket situation was being dominated by scalpers. A group of them, mostly black, huddled outside the room in the hotel where we distributed the tickets. As soon as someone would pick up their tickets, they would be hassled by the scalpers. In some cases, however, deals were struck or had been prearranged. One scalper tried to pick up tickets designated for another person and this led to my being followed into the bathroom. The scalper asked me to change my mind and release the tickets to him. Later, a drunk tried to pick up someone else's tickets and I refused the request. Yelling while leaving the room, he called me an asshole and I felt that it was not necessary for me to accept this treatment. I followed the accuser and his two friends down the hall toward the lobby of the hotel. Confronting the loudmouth, I informed him that his actions were inappropriate and classless, and I was making the effort to help him. After briefly discussing the matter, he apologized for the personal attack. Fortunately, several of the ticket office employees had followed me down the hall, but I had no intention of physically attacking the guy.

While Indianapolis is not one of my favorite sites, we were located in a decent area, but this could not overcome the overall lack of enjoyment on the trip. My personal relationship continued on a downward spiral, aided by the long days and pressure of the tickets. With the hectic pace and frequent phone calls, it seemed to be a good idea for separate rooms for my companion and daughter. With the two rooms and my schedule, we saw little of each other and I sensed there was little that could save the relationship. Despite our closeness, the handling of teenage discipline and my sense of being taken for granted and unappreciated had combined to destroy the enjoyment of living together. Being taken for granted and unappreciated relates closely to greed in my mind, which had grown to be a serious negative for me. They left soon after the school year was over, moving into an apartment in Carrboro, and then later to the house that I had helped her purchase with a contribution to the down payment. They had little furniture and borrowed a number of my pieces, such as barstools and chairs. We remained close and the daughter was an excellent student, MVP of her junior varsity tennis team, and later graduated from Dartmouth.

This brings me up to 2001. I am over thirteen years removed from my last divorce and over four years from the end of my last steady relationship. What was I doing? Trying to find a way to make the days last longer than 24 hours. In '98, I had another blind date and for the first time, I think I was too old. I was 44, she was 32, but part of the problem might have been that I was advertised as mid 30's and once divorced by the person arranging the meeting. She was just officially divorced. In fact, her name changed from the first time I called her until actually getting to meet her. She was attractive, easy to talk to, and I thought we had an enjoyable time, particularly after going to see "There's Something About Mary," an enjoyable comedy. Her name was Mary, which made it all seem funnier. We went out on a Thursday, as she told me she had to work late the next night. She was nice to insist on buying the popcorn and drinks for the movie, so I took her flowers and a card and left them outside her apartment door. Hoping she would be happy to get the flowers after a long day, I also hoped she would at least think I was a decent guy, although incorrectly advertised. I assumed there would be a token thank-you response. Nothing happened for nearly 48 hours, which began to make me worry. She had mentioned that a person meeting the usual crime statistic description had been knocking on doors of several apartments one night recently, looking for a "Maxine." My thoughts ran to stolen flowers or worse, but I tried not to get too negative. I called and left a message and she called back on Tuesday with a nice thank-you and rambling comments about being busy. I tried again, but nothing worked out. Otherwise, I attempted a few other blind dates. One was 36 and quite a fun person, but seriously relationship scarred. Her blind dates and other stories were hilarious. The best was a guy calling her the morning after the initial date and asking to borrow $200. The funny thing was that she said she knew it was coming. Guess he didn't pay for popcorn and drinks. She went out with another guy she had known professionally, and he called to propose the next day. Crazy stuff. She was a delight in person and a great lover of animals with two retrievers and a handicapped cat. The cat eliminated the theory of a female and two dogs.

I am going to stop here, although it is now 2007 as I type this sentence. If this book sells well, I'll do a part two on relationships that includes the internet, long-distance and a reunion. If you are interested, you can help me do part two by getting your friends to buy this book (sounds like a campaign ad).

EPILOGUE

OKAY, SO MAYBE you are pissed off a little by now. You can't say I did not warn you. But, stop for a moment, and tell the truth. Wasn't there something you learned or laughed at? Unless I am completely out of touch with reality, I am betting that you did one or the other. I hope both, but do not want to be overconfident.

At the point of writing this epilogue, I am nearly ten years into this project. This may be the end if sales are too low, or it may be the beginning of a new career. My direction as a writer will be to help keep you informed about the issues of the day. Sure, I'll write with an editorial slant, 'cause that's half the fun. The other half is to stay focused on the world around me, and report it to you. If I have another book(s), I hope you will read it, for as famous filmmaker Ken Burns advised a college class in the spring of 2002, "Read. The book is still the greatest manmade machine of all-not the car, not the PC, I promise."

I have done much of this work on my own, but do want to thank the many people that wrote letters to the editor. It shows there are people that have passion about their feelings and intelligence to match it. If anyone wishes to have their comments removed from the book, I will note this on the book's website. Attempting to contact the many people that were quoted in the book would have significantly delayed the publication. I'll also acknowledge my favorite newspaper, "USA Today" (start printing a weekend sports edition and bring back the late baseball scores), "U.S. News and World Report," "The Week," the many daily newspapers that have contributed stories to this book, and to my friends who have encouraged me by asking when the hell I was going to finish this blasted thing. If I missed acknowledging any source, it was only an oversight, as the amount of research was quite substantial.

When you take a stand on issues of interest, you become a target. I am going on the belief that America is a land of free speech. If there are protests about this book, keep them in perspective. Remember, squeaky wheels don't always get the grease; often they are just damn irritating.

As my favorite musical artist says at the end of his shows, "see you next time."

Made in the USA